MINING MY OWN

THIS MUCH I REMEMBER AND THIS IS HOW I REMEMBER IT

K. B. Chandra Raj

Order this book online at www.trafford.com
or email orders@trafford.com

Most Trafford titles are also available at major online book retailers.

Printed in the United States of America.

ISBN: 978-1-4907-3324-1 (sc)
ISBN: 978-1-4907-3325-8 (hc)
ISBN: 978-1-4907-3326-5 (e)

Library of Congress Control Number: 2014906560

Trafford rev. 06/09/2014

 www.trafford.com

North America & international
toll-free: 1 888 232 4444 (USA & Canada)
fax: 812 355 4082

"Only a fool fixed in his folly may think he can turn the wheel on which he turns"

T.S. Eliot in "Murder in the cathedral"

Contents

Dedication

To my wife of just two winks shy of fifty years who has never failed me.

My soul companion through peak times and trough times, through joys and pitfalls, snarled problems and pratfalls while working for a living, hired, fired and fried in my job just to keep the home fires burning – in three continents consumed by communal killings, tribal warfare, coup d 'e' tats and public hangings; in the throes of all these unsettling vicissitudes and continent hopping she successfully nursed, nourished and nurtured our two children to become accomplished, mature, useful citizens who can hold their own with their peers, Mano- a- Mano anywhere.

She is to the family what the Gibraltar is to the Mediterranean.

And yet may I ask how does one thank fully, do justice, for half a century of kindness, generosity and love in the dedication of a book.

Acknowledgements

My hearty thanks to my caring family and friends in the United States, in far off Kuala Lumpur in Malaysia, Colombo in Sri Lanka, London, Perth and Sydney in Australia, Toronto in Canada, Auckland in New Zealand among many others for encouraging me to keep on writing.

This wood pulp and ink you are leafing through, would not have taken form if not for the Hamden Public Library System, most of all the Whitneyville branch located a chip shot away from my residence, where I measure out my time for four full working days every week.

For me as Jean-Paul Satre so eloquently stated in his erudite work, "Words", "The library was the world caught in a mirror." What Satre who turned down the Nobel Prize in literature believed at a very tender age I have come to realize in my dotage.

He said, "I had found my religion: nothing seemed more important than a book. I regarded the library as a temple."

I would be woefully remiss in my solemn duty therefore if I do not make special mention of Maureen Armstrong the librarian, her amiable and very able assistants, Robert and Pat, for promptly, courteously and successfully fulfilling without failing even once my requests for books, books and more books. Their patience and forbearance is exemplary, worthy of emulation.

As in Dickens's Oliver Twist who plate in hand tearfully pleaded, I too will be back with, "Please sir I want some more."

Author's Note

* Everything stated here is true, although events may not be described in the exact chronological sequence in which they occurred

* I have altered the names of the institutions I worked for in the United States and the names of persons I was associated with in the course of my work

Countries I have lived in

In Asia

Malaysia

Born in Sentul, Malaysia

By land the country borders Thailand, Indonesia and Brunei and by sea Singapore, Vietnam and the Philippines. Malaysia (known before as Federated Malay States) is a member of the Commonwealth of Nations of which the Queen of England is the titular head.

Capital: Kuala Lumpur

Population: Around 29 million

Major racial breakdown: Malays, Chinese, Indians

The constitution declares Islam the state religion while protecting the freedom to practice one's own faith.

Official language: Bahasa Malaysia

Climate: Tropical

1

Ceylon

The country is now known as Democratic Socialist Republic of Sri Lanka. Sri Lanka became independent of the United Kingdom in 1948. It is an island republic in the Indian Ocean, south of India.

Sri Lanka is a member of the Commonwealth of Nations of which the Queen of England is the titular head.

Capital: Colombo

Population: Around 19 million

Major racial breakdown: Sinhalese and Tamils

Official language: Sinhala and Tamil

Climate: Tropical

In Africa

Sierra Leone

The Republic of Sierra Leone in West Africa is bordered by Guinea to the north east, Liberia to the south east and the Atlantic Ocean to the south west

Sierra Leone is a member of the Commonwealth of Nations of which the Queen of England is the titular head.

Capital: Freetown

Population: Around 6 million

Major racial breakdown: Temne and Mende

Official language: English

Climate: Tropical, not humid

Liberia

Situated in West Africa is bordered by Sierra Leone to its west, Guinea to its north and the Ivory Coast to its east

Capital: Monrovia. Named eponymously after James Monroe the 5th president of the United States of America

Population: Around 4 million

Major racial breakdown: Mande, Kru, Mel, Mandigo and Fanti. About 3% of the population is "Americo-Liberians" descendants of freed slaves from the United States of America

Official language: English

Climate: Tropical

Countries visited as accountant

In South America

Suriname

Situated in the northeastern Atlantic coast of South America, Suriname is bordered by French Guiana to the east, Guyana to the west and Brazil to the south.

Capital: Paramaribo

Official language: Dutch

In the Horn of Africa

Eritrea

Bordered by Sudan to the west, Ethiopia in the south and Djibouti to the east

Capital: Asmara

Official language: The country has no official language. The constitution affirms the equality of all Eritrean languages. English serves as a working language. Italian is understood by most people.

How I came to write this book

Soon after my book, *"Your Sense of Humor –Don't Leave Home Without It"* was published my wife planted a chip in my brain which kept buzzing, "You should write about your experiences – you should write about your experiences." While I was kicking the tires about, very reluctant to get into the driver's seat, Mooly, friend from my early accounting years e-mailed me from Toronto, "You should write about your experiences"

I enjoy reading. I can spend hours on end in the company of a book. Poorly tutored in English literature, not in possession of even a piddling knowledge in the art of writing, the woeful want of a university education (the joy of flipping the tassel and tossing the cap in the air eluded me) that would have given me the confidence and cache, the prospect of writing therefore becomes for me a daunting exercise. I take comfort, sustenance, some oxygen from the words of the great Robert Louis Stevenson and move on regardless.

"I think" R.L. Stevenson states, "it improbable that I shall ever write like Shakespeare, conduct an army like Hannibal or distinguish myself like Marcus Aurelius in the paths of virtue." and may I add dribble and shoot goals in soccer like Beckham.

Writing on a particular subject also demands a torrent of reading often not entirely to your liking. Macaulay the renowned scholar reads twenty books to write a sentence; he travels a hundred miles to make a line of description and Samuel Johnson posits that "the greatest part of a writer's time is spent in reading in order to write. He believes "a man will turn over half a library to make a book."

I will be imposing myself on my home town library in Whitneyville for books and more books impinging on their kindness and acts of supererogation ; surfing the internet, scouring Amazon.com (Dave Barry, author of "Insane City" lets us into his modus operandi – "most of my research" he says "consists of Googling in search of factoids that I can distort beyond recognition"), cranking –up my memory; tell me who likes to stir the memory pot?, flexing the memory muscle can be stressful exercise; self-editing, proof reading the publisher's submissions, a frustrating back- and- forth ping pong, in my case all solo and single-handed, a one man band frankly – I might as well be given a pocket knife and ordered to cut up the carcass of a whale – from conception to completion the agony of at the minimum a two year fall from a cliff- pray why do I need this, when I could sunk lazily in the big chair be watching gleefully previous night's recordings of Letterman, Leno or Last Man Standing"

All the while the interminable buzz inescapable and insuperable continued. Right at this time propitious or not independent of my wife's and Mooly's exhortations I got a call from Sid my childhood buddy in New York City, (heaven forbid) "Chandraraj:" he intones *"You should write about your experiences"* and went as far as suggesting a title.

Maybe there is a story to be told, leaping through time colliding with different cultures, crossing oceans and continents, spending nearly all my adult life in countries where I always was a numerical 'minority' and all the insecurities that go with it. The story of an ordinary person propelled by circumstances into great many extra ordinary situations. Hold your applause. The big chair in front of the television was seductively beckoning me and winning.

All I needed at this stage to stop thinking through my fingers and put away my lap top is for one serious person to play ball with me like, "Why do you need this stress?." I was looking for ways to dodge the long hard pull of writing that was staring at me. And so as most of my writing will be undertaken hermetically sealed in this library carrel, on one of my visits to the Whitneyville library hoping I would be shown the rat- hole through which I could hyper drive to freedom, shake off the trammels of the world free to vegetate in solitude and carelessly fleet the time away, I mentioned to the librarian Maureen Armstrong what my wife and old buddies were inveigling me to embark on finishing off with the flourish, "Who the hell is interested in my experiences anyway?" With her usual aplomb and savoir faire she handed me this sobering comment: "If Frank McCourt thought like you we would not have "Angela's Ashes." – The story about a boy struggling with poverty in the slums of Limerick in Ireland. I preferred "Teacher Man" but that's beside the point. The consensus was compelling.

The purpose of this book

The question may be asked if I feared the work would be grim and grueling why then did I decide to write. When Gandhi began writing his autobiography a very close friend had serious doubts. "What has set you on this adventure" he had asked. The friend was very dismissive about the undertaking. The thrust of his question was what purpose would it serve? It is a reasonable question to ask for I too have asked this question.

As every parent knows, children are only mildly impressed by our reckoning of our own fascinating lives until they have children of their own and begin to feel the first twinges, the early heralding of their own advancing age and there is my friend Bob who discouraged me putting it all out. In his opinion it weakens one. It's the secrets that remain untold he says that sustains you. Once you empty yourself you become vacuous and hollow. When revealing one's self he preferred the closed fist to the open palm. I was also painfully conscious that I might hurt the feelings of those close to me but I took comfort from the fact that so long as I stick to facts it should not really matter.

Be that as it may I chose to go for it.

My father left Sandilipay a little village in Jaffna (Ceylon) habited mostly by family, friends and acquaintances, the kind of village where on the day you were born you will know where you will die, who will light the funeral pyre and very often who you will marry. Lives are mapped from birth and nothing you do will alter the map. My father was an aberration - an oddity. When barely eighteen years old when the twentieth century was still in its teens, equipped with nothing more than a high school diploma, a good head for numbers and ability to speak fluently in English threw all discretion to the winds and very likely disregarding wiser counsel my father traveled thousands of miles by boat to take up employment in Federated Malay States (now Malaysia).

How did my grand-parents react to his leaving to settle down so far from home? There was no telephone in his parents' home and letters took several weeks to reach them. How did my father settle down in a country where the population was predominantly Malays and Chinese? Who helped him?

The country was under British colonial rule. The bosses were all British. The Brits lorded over the natives and all non-British down in your sniffling little soul you always saw them as mighty superior. Malcolm Muggeridge in George Orwell's "Burmese Days" gives a clear picture of conditions prevailing at this time.

"Their fatuous insistence on their innate superiority to the "natives", their arid isolation as sahibs in a land which they govern but never bother to understand"

How did the British bosses treat my father handicapped as he was by race, religion and cultural dissimilarity? There prevailed an uncompromising class and color divide.

Consequently the onward and upward movement of his career had predestined limits. Great Britain ruled not only the seas but also the minds of her subjects. They ruled the waves alright but when it came to their kind they were known to waive the rules. I know my father had a trigger – happy temper and we feared his few and far between hair-trigger eruptions. It must have been a prolonged Himalayan endeavor to keep his temper in check at the office. How many trips did he make home to see his parents?

I know he participated in an interstate walking competition and was placed within the first five for which he received a gold chain. He said he would bequeath it to his first grand-son and he did. What was the distance he had to walk? How many participated? I do not know.

How did mother who could not speak English cope? The cultural shock must have been staggering. My mother never worked. It is very likely my parents continued to live in the enclosed way, mentally separate from the more colonial, more racially mixed life around them. So with the salary of a clerk in the Malayan Railways with opportunities for vertical progress cut off beyond a point as plum jobs were set aside for the British – he retired as chief clerk the highest position a non-British could aspire to – how well was he able to provide for the family?

My parents never discussed these matters in my presence. You see as a family we never indulged in cozy talks. They shared in their generation's dread of spontaneity and physical contact. Whatever I learnt growing up about my family was from snatches of conversation I would catch between my parents. Their financial difficulties, health problems, dealings with relatives and even their plans for me were kept away from me by design or default I do not know. I remember my mother one time being very ill and in severe pain. Finally she had to undergo surgery. I visited her at the hospital, kept her company until she was discharged but never knew what she was there for. Many years later I gathered she was operated for tumor of the womb.

I wish I had answers to all the above and more. Elie Weisel in "All Rivers Run to the Sea" referring to his father laments, "How I wish he had told me of his childhood, of his studies and experiences." He goes so far as to say, "Sometimes I envied Isaac, who was alone with his father when he climbed Mt. Moirah." Time and again I have read men and women's refrain of regret that they had not maintained a journal. Here's Gloria Steinem Queen among feminists in "Outrageous Acts and Everyday Rebellions" – "I regret very much, after more than a dozen years of traveling at least a couple of days a week as an itinerant speaker and feminist organizer, that I never kept a diary."

Memories die with their owner and then it's too late to lament, "I wish I had asked my father about that." Again and again we see the second generation having no time to talk to the first.

How I wish my father had maintained a journal. I wish to the best of my ability remedy this omission. My wife is very proud of the book, "Asthma – Cure without Drugs" (now on E-Bay) written by her father, a doctor who qualified in Great Britain which is always at her bedside table. I hope my book will provide a window into the life time experiences of at least one of Neela's and Deeran's progenitors which otherwise would have been lost. This is the goal toward which my sweating horse would strain. I also hope my grandchildren and those who come after them will find this book interesting and even useful even as it gives me the opportunity to remove my mask so I can breathe freely.

A shepherd when asked why he made ritual observances to the moon to protect his flocks replied, "I'd be a damned fool if I didn't." This book, with all its crudities and confusions, contusions and contradictions that could confound even those close to me, frog-leaping in time and space is written for the love of our grandchildren, Neela and Deeran. To echo the shepherd, "I'd be a damn fool if I didn't."

And yet as Maureen Corrigan states in her book, "Leave me alone, I'm reading," "Perhaps there are some life experiences that are simply beyond books."

So sweet Neela and Deeran, "This book's for you."

I begin with a handicap

I do not have the advantage, if I could call it an advantage of a Jean Paul Satre of being born into a family without a father, a Michael Jackson with an abusive father, a George Orwell bearing scars of child abuse, a Sonia Sotomayor's difficult childhood or Oprah Winfrey's well known repeated raping by an uncle. Without unhappy beginnings we would have been deprived of the literary treats such as Samuel Butler's "Way of the Flesh" and Frank McCourt's "Angela's Ashes." These celebrity authors were able to tap the rich vein of the unfortunate circumstances in which they found themselves. Perhaps this is why the Yiddish humorist Sholem Aleichem joked, "I would have given anything for a tiny taste of misery."

It's appropriate to state here Obama's warning in "Dreams from my Father" – "An autobiography promises feats worthy of record, conversations with famous people, a central role in important events. There is none of that here."

There is none of that here too.

No dear reader. I had loving parents who gave freely everything they possessed, financial and emotional for my brother and for me – their only concern was our welfare.

What-ever their limitations those who raised me loved me and did the best they knew how. Of that I am certain. I recall mother telling me "Chandra whatever we own will be split in the middle for the two of you. And that's exactly how it worked out in the end. I am truly sorry for children who do not have cause to love their parents. My parents asked nothing of us. I am wrong. My mother did. Her only request was that my brother and I, our parents' only children should get along. It gives great joy when parents see their grown up kids having fun together more so with their spouses and off springs.

How could I then on whom so much love was lavished justify writing to my brother from the U.S.A. "If something should happen to Ammah or Papa I will not be able to make it" and while working at the Treasury in Sierra Leone I preferred to spend my vacation in the United States rather than visit my aging parents in Ceylon. I never saw them alive again. I will be sorry for this callous and ungrateful indiscretion, a matter of shame and regret I will carry with me till the day I die.

Choice of format

I had great difficulty in choosing the format in which to present what I have to say. I read autobiographies, biographies and memoirs, Helen Keller, Elie Wiesel, Maya Angelou, Obama's "Dreams from my father" and many more at once finishing none. I found it tedious reading. They got into so much detail which did not interest me and I believed it would be the same with my readers too. I've been reading several autobiographies to get me in the mood for writing this book. During the course of these peregrinations I came across three books, "Tesserae" by Denise Levertov, "This Time Together" by Carol Burnett and the delightfully entertaining "Rickle's Book" (by Don Rickles) where the authors recount only memorable incidents in their lives.

The form of this book is that of a Bibiliomemoir. According to Joyce Carol Oates a Bibiliomemoir is a "subspecies of literature combining criticism and Biography with the *intimate confessional tone* of auto biography."

The episodes narrated in this book cover a long expanse of time. So much have I seen and experienced during this period that there is much to dip into. I have chosen only those that seemed to be the most interesting, important, by my reaction self –revelatory and those that seemed to me to have the odor of durability clinging to them.

The Daily Journal

I never maintained a journal and for the purpose of this book I have to rely entirely on memory which in many instances is a blur today. The reason why in most cases, kudos and snubs, joys and pitfalls, surprises and setbacks and how each person met and mastered the challenges he had to face go unrecorded is largely because he is so hell-bent in wringing out a living in a fiercely dog-eat-dog work environment, submerged as it were in the tyranny of everyday anxiety and planning for the future he does not wish to dissipate his energies looking back. Unfortunately only the two-faced Janus was endowed with the ability to see ahead and back at the same time all the time.

Hence you will find me moving from one experience to another like a butterfly that flits from flower to flower; weaving in and out of time, flash forwards and flashbacks, all the time wishing the miracle of remembrance to occur.

The arrangement of the book is by subject matter or by mood or by place, not always by chronology.

How do I feel about life lived so far?

Reader! I exhort you to understand that what you will find here are events hauled from the well of personal experience, of memory pieced together of a past I can recall that has given me pain and pleasure which I have accepted without repining in the spirit of karma as indispensable concomitants of life. As Nietzsche would have it – Amor Fati. For me the route has been long and circuitous whereas for others the path may have been short. It is not the length of the journey that matters as much as the steps we take and the missteps we have made along the way.

Enough time has elapsed to enable me to write clearly without jealousy, sadness, rage, pride or pity clouding my judgment. I bear absolutely no malice having like Saul of Taurus been on the Damascene road for a very long time. When you come to that time of your life as I have when you do not have many more promises to keep and miles to go, the time of life between the twilight at dawn and dawn itself when I can hear the ominous sound of "time's winged chariot drawing near", when the pipe's smoked out, the snuff box's empty, and the turkey buzzards begin wheeling in the sky, it's about time to write what I can recall and write pronto. There is an imminent urgency that is frightfully intimidating. Sometimes I wonder whether some of us have overstayed our welcome on this planet.

I can truly say that many of the joys and sorrows, anger and anguish, rewards and reverses have today lost their poignancy and many incidents in the context of the time of vital importance have been forgotten in the whirl of winding up in one country bidding adieu to friends and familiar surroundings and with palpitating apprehension setting out with my wife and two children to another somewhat less encrusted, like a lobster that has shed its skin and become for a time soft and vulnerable.

Like many millions of aging males I too slipping into my anecdotage have forgotten a great deal. I've lost track of too many details. Shadows lengthen as the sun declines so too as our age advances memory dims. Memory is not a warehouse of finished stories, of neatly framed pictures, not a Mom and Pop hardware shop where every nut and bolt, every pin or piston is tabulated and put in a bin and can be retrieved in two shakes of a lamb's tail. No it's a warehouse of damp and dusty images which needs to be dusted and aired. I do not believe remembering everything is necessary. "Life is not one lived, but what one remembers and how one remembers it in order to recount it." says Gabriel Garcia Marquez in his absorbing book, "Living To Tell The Tale." What one remembers is what happened. There is no past in the absolute. There are only varying versions of the past. Whatever I remember has the potential to reveal something important about me. How I recall them will in all likelihood be different from how others do but what matters to me is how I recall them and what impact it had on my life.

The Trap

I am aware that recounting one's experiences is a responsible undertaking as it can be manipulated in various ways for devious reasons. Andre Aciman in "How memoirists mold the truth" throws plenty of light on this.

"Memoirists, unable to erase the ugliest moments of their life or unwilling to make new ones up, can shift them around. They don't distort the truth, they nudge it. Everyone has reasons for altering the past. We may want to embellish or gloss over the past, or we may want to repress it, or we may shift it just enough so as to be able to live with it."

Certain experiences may be so disturbing one may be tempted to negotiate with the facts for a conscience easing compromise.

This is a trap one can easily fall into.

I shall therefore present in a herky-jerky way a series of sketches, short individual episodes linked together into a narrative and thematic whole, those episodes that I can recall that gave me pleasure or pain taking the precaution to avoid lachrymose pining, self-adulation, self-pity and notably not to be the hero of my story. By no means should this book be a hagiography.

The title

"You best talk to your daughter, Mr. Dunham. White girls don't play with coloreds in this town."

"It's hard to know how much weight to give to these episodes, what permanent allegiances were made or broken, or whether they stand out only in the light of subsequent events. Whenever he spoke to me about it, Gramps would insist that the family left Texas in part because of their discomfort with such racism. Toot would be more circumspect; once, when we were alone, she told me that they had moved from Texas only because Gramps wasn't doing particularly well on his job, and because a friend in Seattle had promised him something better. According to her, the word racism wasn't even in their vocabulary back then." "Dreams from My Father" - Barack Obama

The reader will observe different reasons have been adduced for the grandparents leaving Texas - the grandfather's, the grandmother's and Obama's own understanding of it. We are left wondering which version is to be taken seriously. This is nothing new. Many writers of autobiographies and memoirs rely on friends and relatives to fill-in memory gaps.

In order not to adulterate my narrative by conjecture and contradictory recollections by friends and family and, to stay true to the title- this much I remember and this is how I remember it – I have relied entirely on my memory. What I don't remember did not happen.

My Story

Everyone has a story to tell. Each person's experience is unique. It is singularly different from that of the next person. He alone feels the full weight and thrust of his experiences – the angst and the agony of disappointment, the ecstasy and exhilaration that accompany success.

It's true I lived in absolute dread in Malaysia as a little child when the Japanese soldiers ran roughshod over the country committing unspeakable crimes, the heads of errant locals cut and spiked on poles like pig's head on a stick, put out on busy streets for all to see for which the soldiers were accountable to no one.

Worked for a living in Ceylon, a country that was for over four decades raked over the coals of internecine warfare born out of fierce hatred between two communities fomented by self-seeking politicians resulting in the deaths of innocents in the thousands, destruction of property and the displacement of families from their natural homes, a diaspora "Made in Sri Lanka." Is this why Bishop Heber described Ceylon (now Sri Lanka) as a country "where every prospect pleases and man alone is vile." I had ring-side view of a new world replacing an old one, a new world in which my family had no place.

Lived in Sierra Leone where many Brits lured by the glitter of gems in arid Kono would go to but few would return laid low by the malaria carrying anopheles mosquito – "the white man's grave" they called this West African state. In Sierra Leone deep in the woods I saw in a shabby dark ill ventilated shack a little kid no more than say ten years with the look of terror, eyes wide open, mouth agape brought in minutes after genital mutilation, she having surrendered ceremoniously but unwillingly the autonomy over her own private parts.

Lived in Liberia during the time of the bloody coup engineered by the president's personal body guard, Master Sargent Samuel K Doe and, as if though that wasn't enough Samuel K. Doe assassinated president William Tolbert even after it was widely reported he had on bended knees begged to be spared, and then publicly executed ministers of state, one of whom was my neighbor.

The race of man even after centuries of civilization, still holds to some traits of its barbarous barbarian forefathers.

Here I am now in the United States having made a giant leap from third to the first world, an escape from one sphere to another, living in a country where one relies more on pluck than luck, with horizons broadened, becoming more self-reliant in order to survive.

America knocks the nonsense out of you.

During these inter- continental gypsy years working to support my family I was hired and fired from jobs in rapid fire. Career wise I have worn many suits, and not all of them had been a good fit. I served many bosses one different from the other as chalk is to cheese, as caviar is to French fries. You will want to read what I think of them in a separate section of this narrative. They are a good sample of humanity regardless of class, caste, color or physiological contours. They are the same everywhere – Asia, Africa or the U.S.A.

My regret

I wish I could enrich these reflections with the names of all those, the many who have ministered to my happiness and that of my wife and children. Alas it's very likely they may never cross our paths again in this life but let me assure them as Helen Keller did, "that the influence of their calm mellow natures is a libation poured upon our discontent and we always feel its healing touch, as the ocean feels the mountain stream freshening its brine." Pray how else could my family have survived crisscrossing continents for years and I, hopping from one billet to another. As "iron sharpens iron" I sincerely hope I have been of some help to them. There will always be a bond between us that cannot be sundered by time, distance or death for that matter for I know we shall meet on the other side of the shore. I have lost friends, some by death, some through indifference to reach out my electronic hand.

"Just the facts Ma'am

All we want are the facts"

Joe Friday

My father comes to school

It must have been around ten in the morning when I casually looked out of my class room. To my surprise there was my father talking to my teacher out on the corridor. I did not know what to make of it. I do not remember him ever coming to my, the Batu Road School for whatever reason. If he had any business to conduct he would have ordinarily gone directly to the office, attended to matters and returned to work. This was most unusual. I could not hear what they were talking about. I remember father was in white slack, white short-sleeve shirt and tie. He used to then sport a Hitler mustache. The conversation was brief. The teacher came up to me and said words to the effect your father wishes to speak with you. You may leave the class. When I went up my father said, "Today will be your last day at school. Say goodbye to your friends. We leave for Ceylon next week." He said it as casually as he would sometimes say to me after supper, "Chandra let's go buy durians." He then dipped into his pocket and gave me some change. Good enough to blanja a friend at the Tuck Shop with a bowl of meehoon and a cup of ice cream.

And he was gone.

Elmo Jumeaux and I during lunch time would play marbles or sit on the concrete bench and shoot the breeze until the bell separated us. Lunch time I gave my dear friend the news. We hugged and kissed and departed. At this moment that we will walk different paths, will meet new friends and may never meet again never occurred to me. We promised to write but never did. Often I think of him and wonder where he is now.

Sayonara to Sentul

I was playing cricket. I was batting at that time when a domestic help comes up to me and says, "Ammah wants you home." I dropped the bat and went along. All the things were packed and poised for dispatch. In a couple of hours we left.

My father, my mother and I left for Ceylon by steamer, "S.S. Samaria." My brother had departed three months earlier by Arundale Castle, the first steamer to set sail after the war. I occupied a cabin about a foot above the water line and I spent a good while looking through the port hole at the capricious ocean. On the way a hat that my father bought and cautioned to be very careful blew away for the breeze when I looked out of the train window as the train was pulling out of the station. From then on whenever father gave me anything for safe-keeping he would remind me, "Don't lose this the way you lost the hat."

Thus I said Sayonara to my birth place and so began my odyssey through three continents, from Malaysia to Ceylon, Sierra Leone, Liberia, Eritrea, Surinam and the U.S.A where I now reside permanently with my wife, Siva.

Of one thing I am certain. Life takes you where you didn't plan to go.

Victor and I

Victor and I were close buddies. We attended Batu Road School in the town, feeder to the prestigious Victoria Institution, about seven miles away traveling by bus. He lived a few blocks away. I would be given money (cannot recall how much) sufficient to get me a bowl of meehoon and ice cream. Sometimes I shared my meehoon with Victor. And my mother would know. After supper (nothing of consequence was taken up before supper) I would be grilled as to whether I had shared my lunch money. Of course I would deny it and mother would say "I know Chandra, I know- mothers have a way of knowing these things"

After persistent, prolonged and patient ferreting I would confess, "I shared my lunch money with Victor." "Next time don't lie because Ammah can see from here." How did she know? Dear God. My appetite at supper time fluctuated.

The Barber of Sentul

The visceral attraction of a bicycle to children is universal and timeless. The feeling of freedom and achievement in learning to ride the tumultuous way with falls and bruises and back again trying and finally subduing the monster and thereafter like Edmund Hilary to Tensing after Mount Everest to be able to say, "We have conquered the bastard" is exhilarating. In those days this was the first solo combat a child engaged in. Alas now with the invention of the training wheel children are deprived of the quixotic thrill of battle with the bicycle we would recall nostalgically in later years. Learning to ride a bicycle was a way of escaping restlessness at home.

It was in Sentul that I learnt to ride a bicycle. The barber made house calls. He came on a fixed Sunday of the month. I would gather that the barber is expected from the preliminary arrangements that will be made. The chair that was always used for this purpose would be dusted and placed in the usual position in the atrium. I had other plans. When he came to practice his tonsorial artistry on my father I would take his bicycle and be on my way. The bike was of course too big for me. So I placed my feet below the bar and holding the bar with my right arm I would pedal about hundred yards back and forth down the street. The barber too was from Ceylon and so my father and he had a lot to talk about. If I got late to bring the bicycle back which was often my father and the barber would be standing outside the house looking out for me. Not once did either of them display any irritation. Standing outside they would continue talking.

Confident now in my ability to ride I would occasionally unbeknownst to my parents rent a bicycle and ride along the main road. I can recall the shop where I rented the bicycle. A small shop with a low roof and dimly lit on the main road. How I was able to convince the owner to rent it to me, a little fellow, I do not have the foggiest idea. Father soon came to know of this through a friend who had seen me riding on the busy main road and put a stop to it. I was not punished. My father believed I was too puny and would not survive the kind of beating he could dish out. He is supposed to have said that to my mother. That may not be all. When my father was mad and grabbing the cane called out for me I would with drooping head go up to him like cattle to the slaughter house or better a condemned to the scaffold and passively submit myself for punishment. He then would feel sorry for me and say "Get out of here." With my brother it was different. No sooner father seized the cane my brother would take to his heels and a chase would follow with not so very pleasant consequences.

My visit to Kuala Lumpur

My father had a brother and two sisters living with their families in Malaysia. The brother lived in Taiping, a sister in Ipoh and the other sister in Kuala Lumpur. I do not remember visiting the brother in Taiping or the sister in Ipoh. I remember very well my visit to my aunt's home in Kuala Lumpur. It was a commodious house and several coolies would all the time be tending to the garden. There was a fair distance between the living rooms and the dining room. A bell would be sounded summoning us to meals.

On the day I arrived (my brother did not accompany me on this visit) after supper my aunt and family retired as must have been their custom to the master bed room leaving me all alone in the drawing room. I could hear the family laughing, having a merry time. Seated in the chair I cried. I missed home. I must have fallen asleep.

Moments of childhood lodge in our memory for diverse reasons – beauty, drama, comedy and sometimes some things so painful they tenaciously hang on without letting go of their grip.

The swamis next door

There was a couple living next door on Railway View road. They had no children. I would spend some of my free time in this house. My parents were on good terms with them but I do not remember any neighborly visits either way. Theirs' was the end house. My mother was very friendly with the ladies in other homes down the street. Soon after the husbands leave for work by train and the cooking done the ladies would get together in any one home and swap stories. At noon the ladies would rush back to their homes to receive their husbands coming to lunch. The men had just about half an hour to spare and then they have to catch the return train back to work. From our house I can see the train go by. Soon after, the ladies met again till four O'clock and disperse in time to welcome their husbands. My mother would be so absorbed in the jabber that often I have to hold her cheek and ask, "Can I go out to play?" Paying scarce attention to what I was saying she would reply "yes" and carry on laughing and gesticulating. Not satisfied I would hold her cheek again and ask, "Now look at me and say properly, "yes". Even this at times did not work. There have been times when she has asked, "Who gave you permission to go out and play?"

I digress - Back to our neighbor. Swamis of the Hindu faith visited this home. There were more of them during weekends. Seated in a circle on the floor, saffron-robed they would sing thevarams (Hindu religious verses) and smoke a clay pipe after first wrapping the mouth piece with a piece of cloth. The pipe would be passed around and each swami would take a hearty pull. I would listen to their singing and watch the smoking with reverence. When I asked what they were smoking I was told "it's a heavenly product". Once a swami gave me some seeds and said, "Plant these in a flower pot and when the plant grows big bring me the leaves. Growing them in your house will bring you good luck" he said.

I had a great deal of respect for these swamis. They sang well and were always in a jolly mood. A friendly lot really. I have a hot and cold relationship with religion and piety. During this period I was really hot. I did as instructed. I planted the seeds in a flower pot with utmost care, watered it and watched over it. Every morning on getting up I would go over and check to see how much the plants had grown. I reported to the swamis regularly the progress and on a couple of occasions plucked and passed on the leaves to them.

My uncle who was always effusively received and heartily welcomed in our home and with whom I would stay briefly on my return visit to Sentul many years later, a police officer in Kuala Lumpur visited us. "Where on earth did you get these plants?" he inquired of my mother. My mother told him exactly how it happened. "This is ganja. If you are caught possessing this you will be sent to jail." The plants were swiftly destroyed and I was forbidden to visit the neighbor.

I overheard my parents talk that the lady next door short and buxom and forever chewing betel gave birth to a swami-like baby. The lady impressed me as thoroughly good and honest, naïve and not very bright.

The Japanese are here

Dating back to 10,000 B.C. the Japanese culture by all accounts rich and diverse is greatly admired and widely respected. The flowing graceful kimono, the rituals of the Sado tea and the Kado incense ceremonies, the Kabana flower arrangement, the Origami art of folding paper, the Bonsai method of growing miniature trees, the healthy tradition of removing soiled shoes when entering a house and wearing clean slippers, greeting respectfully bowing waist down instead of shaking hands, hygienically a welcome practice speak very highly of the Japanese way of life.

This is not what I witnessed when the Japanese occupied Malaysia after they drove the British away. Heavy handed in all their dealings with the natives they ran rough shod over the country. This is world war 11. Overnight the use of English was forbidden. All government business was conducted in Japanese. Name boards and street signs were changed to Japanese, a language no one understood. "Hurry-up and learn Japanese" we were warned. I know my father and his friends feared going to work. This I gathered from his discussions with neighbors. Father and I studied Japanese from the same primary book, at different times of course.

The British currency was withdrawn from circulation and in its place Japanese paper currency was introduced. Inflation rose like a hydrogen-filled balloon. Not dissimilar to Germany during the Weimar Republic in 1923 when the Germans carried their money in wheel barrows when going shopping. Any time the government needed money it resorted to the printing press. I remember my father and me carrying a large brief case filled with paper money to buy grocery. Although it was a capital offense to have British money people confident the British will take back Malaysia hoarded it secretively. A close relative once brought a trunk-full of British currency for safe-keeping. I remember father telling him he should lock the trunk and take the key away. The trunk was placed under the bed. I was never told how he came by so much money. May be that he was a police officer had something to do with it.

Under Japanese occupation children seldom left their homes for fear of incurring the wrath of Japanese soldiers. When you encounter a soldier you should bow waist down or risk being slapped. I heard my father tell my mother that a friend of ours had walked past a Japanese sentry – there were armed soldiers at every junction – and unaware of the soldier's presence the friend did not bow. He was called over and slapped. Mind you he had to walk up to him to be slapped. With difficulty I would persuade my mother to allow me to play cricket or badminton on the gravel road outside the house. Word came to us while playing that two men in the nude were being paraded on Main Avenue. A few of us sneaked up and saw two large men being taken down the road hand-cuffed and in the nude by a Japanese soldier and a local carrying a placard on which was written "These two men were caught stealing an officer's car; If you steal this will happen to you too." This was of course in English. We understand they were taken to the Railway Station and during rush hour beaten to death in full sight of the commuters. This is how it is done. Soap water is pumped into the stomach and when the stomach gets bloated you are beaten till you die. My father said it was a familiar sight to see heads spiked on poles along the road. Older children had to attend Japanese classes. In one instance a child seated at the back of the class was caught combing his hair. The heads of all children in the class were shaved bald. One child who suffered this fate lived next door.

I remember playing down the street right outside our house and espied a Japanese soldier with a sword dangling on his side- they all carried swords – walking towards us. My father was at work. My mother was at home. We were playing cricket. I was terrified. I dropped the bat and ran into our house. He stopped in front of the house, thought for a while and then climbed up the stairs and walked on to the verandah. I was too excited or too afraid to lock the door. There was on the wall a religious picture. He looked at it questioningly. I said to him "God, God". He gave me a cold stare and repeating something that sounded "Gawd-Gawd" walked away. My mother knew nothing of what occurred. My father decided it was not safe to stay on where we were. The house was close to the Central Workshop where rail carriages and engines were serviced and repaired. Soldiers were a common sight here. They were free to do whatever they liked. No action could be taken against them. They were a law unto themselves. So father moved to a solitary house in a wooded area. To me it looked like a jungle. How he came by that house I do not know. The place was called Sungaituwa. There were no other houses nearby. It was very lonely here, even scary. To get provisions we had to trudge a long distance. My father gets antsy when his routine is disrupted. When I was married and living in Colombo whenever he visited us we could feel his impatience to get back home to familiar surroundings. From the jungle of Sungaituwa father brought us back to our old house on Railway View road in Sentul.

Now when I think about it the brutal behavior of the Japanese should not surprise us. Was it not the Japanese who introduced to the world *Kamakazi* ("God's Wind") – the pilot crashing his plane into the funnel of a war ship thereby destroying it and in the process take his life – precursor to the Al Qaeda suicides. It is well known the Japanese officer would rather commit *Hara Kiri* (disemboweling with a sword) than be taken a prisoner. The Japanese General who was in charge of administering Malaysia committed *Hara Kiri* rather than surrender to the British.

No sense of direction

From Railway Institute road close to the club where father played tennis and I had my love affair with table tennis, we moved to a slightly larger house two parallel roads away on Railway View road. The day after we moved I got ready in the evening to go to the club and was about to leave when I heard my father ask my mother, "Does Chandra know the way to get home?" I ignored the question and, with that exaggerated confidence that springs from ignorance I left for the club post haste. There was just one road, the Main Avenue separating Railway Institute road where the club was situated and Railway View road where I now lived. They ran parallel. I did not know the way back home. I ran up and down Main Avenue banging two four inch sticks for company, more and more up and down Main Avenue and it was now beginning to get dark. I was afraid. I could have gone to any one of the houses on Main Avenue and asked. I did not just as a driver lost in a city is loath to ask for directions. I reached out to that friend of all children in distress, whimper. A gentleman stopped and asked why I was crying and I replied I do not know the way home. Whose son are you he wanted to know. Kanagarajah I replied and he brought me home to my parents. Thereafter I had to accompany father to and from the club.

The British retake Malaysia

Then the bombings began. When the planes were sighted the sirens would go off. If it was during day time we would get into the shelter built outside the houses on the side walk. Malays, Chinese, Indians and other nationalities I cannot remember hid in these shelters which were covered. Prayers in different languages, a cacophony really, were sung aloud in these trenches. How god-fearing, good and holy we become when our well-being is threatened. We heard bombs fall all around us. When the planes, I remember well the B twenty ones, turned back the long all clear siren would be sounded and we would emerge from the shelter. During the day we would not know whether father was safe as he would be at work about ten miles away and there was no way of communicating with him. Anxiously we would await the train to bring him home. Tomorrow is another day of tension, tenterhooks and uncertainty.

If the bombings occurred during the night we were instructed to get under the bed. I can see the trunk with the money. Our house was about half a mile from the Central Workshop which the British were anxious to put out of commission. Very often they missed the mark and civilian homes were bombed resulting in many deaths.

The euphemism is collateral damage. I remained inside the shelter but my brother would walk up to the entrance and peep out to see bombs coming down he said like a bunch of grapes.

Subhash Chandra Bose

While in Malaysia I had the distinct honor of seeing the well- known Indian patriot and Freedom Fighter affectionately called, "Netaji." Chandra Bose was all for driving the British away from India through force, militarily. Placed under house arrest by the British he escaped in 1941 with Japanese help and with their encouragement he organized the Indian National Army. I have witnessed soldiers of the Indian National Army march in Sentul in their colorful uniforms. When Bose visited Sentul where he was a high value guest of the Japanese government the students were requested to assemble on the grounds to hear him speak. I was seated on the grounds barely ten feet away.

Post World War

The war was now over. Life began to get normal and schools began to function like before. Friends, relatives and neighbors commenced living as they had before Japanese occupation. People rejoiced. Those of us who were born and grew up under British colonial rule were comfortable under the British. English was the medium of instruction in schools. We looked up to the British and tried hard to emulate them. Speak, write and behave like them. We were taught to begin every letter, "I am by the grace of God in the *pink* of health and hope you are the same." Pink of health? We would write so even though some of us were darker than mid night and can never turn pink come what may. In class we were taught *one swallow does not make a summer* although I would not have recognized a swallow even if one perched and peed or pooed on my head.

Under the British there prevailed harmony of the kind we saw in the flick, *Driving Miss Daisy*. The black driver knew his place and served the white woman loyally. So long as you do not challenge the system, make waves or attempt to rise above your station, you will be alright. In my father's office the bosses were all British. The ruler-ruled, master-servant attitude prevailed. It is noxious atmosphere to live and work in for it deprives one of self-esteem, retards

47

development, cripples natural curiosity and stunts one's personality. This reminds me of the way the caste system operated in the Northern part of Ceylon. So long as the so-called "lower caste" or *Harijans* (children of God) as Gandhi would later refer to them accepted their inferior station in life all was well.

The War on Me

The four and a half years or so of no schooling had a tremendous deleterious lasting impact on my life. When it was time for me to start schooling and was put age-wise with my peers I always lagged behind in perception which resulted in my always having a creepy fear of tests. The fact that immediately at the end of this prolonged absence of studies of any kind I was put in a hostel where studies were not supervised, no guidance of any kind further compounded the chronic problem. Disheartened I believe, I never worked on catching up which more resourceful kids would have done.

The enjoyment that comes from reading books like Hardy Boys, The Treasure Island and Gulliver's Travels passed by me like "black-out" ships during the war in the night. No museums, no magicians and no clowns. The closest I came to edification, or diversion or laughter was when my cousin during war time would tell us stories from books she had read. Justice Sonia Sotomayor in her autobiography, "My beloved World" recalls that she never heard of "Alice in Wonderland" until she got to Princeton years later. Good for her. From among the millions only very few come through the sieve nice and clean like the good Justice.

Here's what Jean Paul Satre says in this context.

"Every man has his natural place; its altitude is determined by neither pride nor value: childhood decides."

My mother was not English literate. She conversed with the indigenous folks in Malay. I recall there were occasions after supper my father would teach me some arithmetic. He was preoccupied like all his peers trying real hard to cope with the big changes that were taking place in our lives. I do not recall seeing books lying around which I could have peered into. Today's children who are not prone to reading are able to look at the world and learn a lot through the window which is the television. There was no television at this time.

My parents loved my brother and me dearly and would have gone to any length to see we got a sound education. Equally important parents should take pains to create an atmosphere, an environment in the home wherein the child will want to go for higher education.

Me and exams

I fared very badly at examinations. I dreaded examinations. I would approach them full of dark and gloomy foreboding. Shakespeare captures my mood with precision. I hoped little by little my abilities will catch up with my ambitions but they never did.

This is how I would feel before each exam.

"Between the acting of a dreadful thing

And the first motion, all the interim is like a phantasma

Or a hideous dream"

Paralyzed by fear I would forget even the little I knew. The thought of examinations gave me the collywobbles. And then comes the feeling, after all, all I can do is fail and damn it failure loses much of its sting over time. I knew not only how to fall and fail I knew how to get up. I've done it so often. I had by and by, bit by bit made peace with diminished expectations.

Failure at exams did not follow me like a shadow. It presaged me. It was the dreaded precursor; waited for me and bear-hugged me on arrival. My aptitude could never catch up with my ambitions. Any-thing I touched by way of exams turned to dross - A Midas touch in reverse. A sense of strain, of nerving my-self for the hangman's noose got hold of me by the throat as the date of the examination crept closer. Barely a month to go having had only a nodding acquaintance with the text book my heart sickened at the labors ahead of me.

This might sound dippy to the reader but I had no choice. There was going to be an 'end of term test'. I cannot recall what subject it was. I was totally unprepared; nothing strange about that. There was no purpose going for it. I would have had to submit a blank sheet or close to it. I had to find a way. I went into a close huddle with my- self; undertook a cost – benefit analysis and came to a decision. I rook a razor with my left hand and slashed my right fore-finger. With a massive bandage like a Sikh's turban I went to the hostel warden and said it was an accident and obtained an "excuse chit" to stay away from the test.

I failed the Ceylon University entrance examination twice in all the subjects. At this time there was only one university in the whole of Ceylon (there are eight I understand in the Connecticut New Haven County alone) and every mother's son and daughter was fiercely competing for a place. The enterprising, dedicated ones were rewarded. As for me at the end of it all I feel a manqué. A man or woman must have a sound academic qualification to cling to. Without that I now have come to the painful realization, pretty late don't you think, he will forever as I have been be a pea vine struggling in search of a trellis.

I never met an exam I liked.

In Ceylon

Now in our village Chankanai the family congress decided that my brother and I should be sent to a boarding school and my parents would return to Malaysia. I overheard this when I was lying in bed with eyes closed and relatives and my parents discussing the next move for my brother and for me. My brother and I were to be admitted as boarders at Jaffna College (College in Ceylon is high school in the U.S.) a well- recognized institution in the Northern part of Ceylon established in 1867 by American missionaries. This was a mistake. It took my mind completely off studies. I decided to participate in all the sports activities in full measure. While others were studying I went for boxing classes.

I recall my brother and I being taken to the Chunnakam railway station and there from the platform I could see my parents go away, recede into the distance. I hugged the station pillar and cried. There was a gnawing at the intestines. I felt abandoned. I did not understand the need to be so insensitive. I could see my mother looking out of the window until I could not see her anymore. "Love knows not its depth until the hour of parting."

My wife and I almost committed this unpardonable "crime" on our daughter. Fortunately for her and for us we did not. We were returning to Ceylon from Liberia after the coup where we half-heartedly planned to settle down for good. At this time in Ceylon the medium of instruction at schools was in the vernacular, Sinhalese or Tamil depending on to which ethnic division you belonged. We were very keen that our daughter should be taught in English. There was one way this could have been achieved. Send her to a school in Kodai Canal in South India. So we detoured on our return journey to Ceylon and visited this school, spoke to the principal who happened to be from Ceylon and he was agreeable to admitting her at the appropriate time. We discussed this with my wife's father, a doctor regarding medical certificates and inoculations and reviewed the finances too. Then close to the time we just could not make up our minds to part with our daughter. Sometimes sentiment and emotion prevail over sensibility for the better. Tough love took a knock- out blow. A black-eye!

Memories of Jaffna College

The food:

I was in the boarding. The food was never enough and what was put out was barely edible. We were young and always hungry. When I saw on the television the University of Connecticut Basket Ball player telling the reporter that he goes nightly hungry to bed I knew exactly what he meant. Any time I came across some money I would spend it on bread and sambol in the nearby boutique. If a little flushed I would spend it on cocoa at the Tuck Shop. The names of boarders who have mails will be posted on the library notice board. The recipient can go in and collect his letter. Lunch time I would go and look feverishly at the notice board. Father very often would include some money with his letters. Money was always used to buy food and nothing else. At times I walked over to my brother living in the senior hostel to inquire whether he could spare some money. In life it's always like this: You win some you lose some. You catch some you miss some. But try you must.

Almost the same rice and curry would be there. No second service allowed. On Sundays we were given a pinch of meat. Well before the dining hall opened there would be a line formed outside. If you are late you can kiss your meat 'Good Bye.'

Right in front of us at a long table the teachers would be served their meals, a variety and plenty of it. On one occasion on a week day while school was in session the same rice and curry was repeated for the third consecutive day. There were plenty of grumbling and then we heard a senior call out "strike." We all without exception walked out leaving the food untouched. The day scholars who heard this rushed home and brought us biscuits. The boarding master was furious. He sent word that if we did not come back to the dining table we would all be sacked. Here in the United States we would say "fired"

With heads bowed we returned to our seats and having nibbled a bit went back to class. I do not recall any other strike during my stay at the Jaffna College hostel.

We all looked forward to the long week-ends for different reasons. Some pining for the pampering by parents when they get home and some plotting to stay behind as during this time there will be no studies and no early rising. I would make a very strong case why I should stay behind. "Why is it chandraraj everyone wants to go home except you and you live so close by." the warden would ask. "My grandparents are very old and they are in no state of health to look after me." I would reply. They would have gladly accommodated me feeding me with juicy mangoes. There was much more fun in unsupervised life at the hostel.

Into sports

In the boarding with no one checking on my progress in studies I went gung-ho for sports. I played cricket, representing the junior college team against St. John's college; opened batting at twelve O'clock noon and at tea time four O'clock was not out having scored forty runs; represented the junior college in soccer, played field hockey and boxing. So at Jaffna College or in any other college in Ceylon or elsewhere I never won any prizes for studies. The return from success in sports is instant – the cheers and adulations unlike from success in exams where the gestation period is inordinately prolonged. When at the end of term the school gathered and names of prize recipients would be called out my name would be mentioned for only winning the Table Tennis tournament. The honorees go up to the stage and receive the prize from the principal. Sadly the stage evokes unpleasant memories for me. For the first time, never again, I witnessed a student receiving a public caning for having assaulted a student prefect of the school.

Escaped a beating

At the Junior Hostel (boarding) I was elected president. There were junior, senior and girls' hostels and each elected a president to hold office for a year. End of year each hostel would have a party and the president would be invited. In my hostel was this guy who was much older and bigger. He had no business to be there. He should have been with the bigger boys in the senior hostel. How he was allowed to be with much younger students I do not know. He was not well disposed towards me as his favorite lost the election to me.

During lunch time when I was out in the lawn chatting with friends, using some excuse or other he challenged me and was on the point of giving me a sound beating. News got to my brother in the senior hostel close by. In a flash my brother arrived and challenged the bully and in the verbal fisticuff that followed the whole matter fizzled out. I had no problem with him thereafter.

That ties of close family relationships must be honored and sustained in the conduct of human affairs is sacrosanct.

My uncle in Vavuniya

While my parents were in Malaysia I was required to spend the school vacation with either one of my mother's two brothers. This time it was with my mother's older brother who worked for the Government Railways in Vavuniya.

In the evenings I would visit the club and spend time there. I saw on the club notice board there was going to be a Table Tennis tournament which required a very small entrance fee. I put my name down, played the matches and won the championship. I was presented with a trophy. My uncle was unaware of this. I was going to surprise him. So with the trophy in hand, head held high, I headed for home. As I approached the house I could hear my uncle's angry words like a peal of thunder. "Where did this fellow learn all this cheating habits?" He was holding my school report card in his hand. The report card mentioned the fact that I was caught cheating.

This is what happened:

In my class I was good in English but atrocious in arithmetic. So with the student seated next to me at end of term test a deal was stuck. He would drop the arithmetic answer paper on the floor; I would pick it up copy the answers and drop it back on the floor. The same would be done by me with the English essay answer.

My "friend" dropped the arithmetic answer on the floor. I casually picked it up and placed it on the table to copy. Just then the supervising teacher who was observing all this came up to the table took both answer scripts and made his comments and we were asked to proceed.

There now at my uncle's house I stood trophy in hand cowed and bowed, stripped naked of my *amour – propre* bereft of all self -respect while my uncle went into a paroxysm of anger. To this day I can see myself standing there with shame and shock when I should have been looked upon admiringly as a visiting conqueror.

Concerning my birth

After I was married my mother mentioned this one incident to my wife in my presence, the only time she drew aside the veil and allowed us a peep into their parlous pecuniary past. This happened in Malaysia. My mother was expecting me and my parents did not have sufficient money for medical expenses. Tamil parents went to great lengths to see their sons educated and their daughters married off with handsome dowry comprising mostly of good-size jewelry of the twenty four carat gold variety and some real estate. The education of girls during this time was glossed over. The girl should marry a doctor or a lawyer, need not become one. Man was the provider and protector; women served and deferred. In the event the husband died early without adequate savings the wife could fall back on the proceeds from the sale of the "dowried" assets for her sustenance as a last resort. Very seldom widows married again. A husband worth his salt would never lay his hands on his wife's dowry. It was passed on to one's progeny by and by.

My mother did what a Hindu Tamil woman would seldom do since it is a tacit acknowledgement that the family has hit rock bottom. She offered my father some of her jewelry given as dowry by her parents to be pawned. My father she said left home but returned with the jewelry. He had walked up and down it seems in front of the pawn shop but could not make up his mind to enter it to "commit the crime." We'll manage" he's supposed to have said. How he managed is what I would like to know.

This much I know having been raked over the coal of career uncertainties, highs and lows, the head of the family like the captain of a vessel in a storm must navigate his ship to safe harbor.

Financially and psychologically it must have been one enormous strain and there is so much agony and anxiety one goes through in life that cannot be converted to words. We do not live in the external world of sticks and stones, bricks and mortar but in the phantasmagoric chamber of our tormented brain.

Representing Ceylon in India

I was selected to represent Ceylon in Table Tennis in India. I was thrilled – what many call a "chance of a life time." The Table Tennis Association was barely solvent. So it was agreed by the Central Committee that the Association would pay for travel, the host country the hotel expenses and the cost of the blazer with the emblem on it by members of the team. My father had retired and was receiving a fixed pension. He had two children to educate. I go up to my mother- I remember vividly she was seated in the white rattan chair in the living room, very popular in Malaysia- and give her the good news first that I have been selected to represent Ceylon and the association and others will bear the *entire* cost *except* the cost of the blazer. She knew what was coming and went mute. "Houston" I thought even then "we have a problem." After what I thought was a life time she asked, "How much?" I replied, "one hundred and twenty five rupees Ammah." More deafening silence! I was now silently sniping, "surely-surely"

My mother would save from the monthly house expense allowance my father would give her. She would keep them within the folds of her saree in the wardrobe. I went to India as a member of the Ceylon team. What she had planned to do with that money I will never know. I did not care. It never passed through my mind at that time. I just took the money and bolted. I recall now with sadness, gratitude and chagrin, the anguish that was written all over her face while mentally taking count of how much money there might be within the folds of her saree.

The games were played in Shaharanpur in the northern most part of India. Our residence was as per the road sign fifty miles from the base of the Himalayan range. Yes it was very cold. No electric heaters. A fire place "to go round" we would have difficulty to get the tooth paste out of the tube. By the time we got warmed up the game would have been over.

Considering the fact the money my parents had to spend, relying solely on a pension was exiguous and inelastic it must have driven them to resort to extreme austere measures. The only words my mother uttered were "How much?" No more.

As children we feel so much but are able to feel so little for others.

'Tis true the tangible umbilical cord that connects the mother to the child is severed at birth but it's replaced by an endearing emotional cord, "the silver cord" that is more enduring.

On my return from India I wanted to be a star player like those I saw, Thiruvengadam especially, a defensive player from Madras, south India. The cheers and the adulation of spectators went straight to my head and I was dizzy. To be in that league I knew I had to put in long hours of practice. I could not have done it while studying for exams. So I went up to my mother soon after my return and said to her I wanted to give up studies. I remember this incident so well.

Nary a word she walked up to the stack of fire wood in the kitchen, picked up one and said to me not very politely and not softly, "I do not want to hear about giving up studies again in this house." That was the last time I brought the subject up.

My visit to the hospital

My father was at the General Hospital in Colombo after cataract surgery where I would visit him regularly. I was successful in getting the job as accountant in a British firm on a handsome salary with health benefits, two generous bonuses a year and many other fringe benefits. An executive position in a British firm had cachet. I had not completed the final part of the Chartered accountancy exam. My friends had and were now in good jobs. Bachelors all, plenty of money and no studies to worry about they were having a grand time eating in posh restaurants, going to plays and concerts, balcony seats at movies the imprimatur of success. I was anxious to join them in the fun and so did the risky thing (as you will see from now on taking risks becomes my only safety net) of accepting the job without completing the finals.

So on my visit to the hospital to see my father still on a fixed pension by no means princely, I said to him, "Papa I have accepted a very good job with a fine salary and benefits." He looked at me with one eye, the other bandaged and said in a serious tone showing no signs of relief on being released from financial responsibilities, none what so ever, "Chandra" he said, "as long as you want to study I will find the money" My parents' best trait was their devotion to the education of their children at whatever cost physical, financial.

It was thus the financial umbilical cord between father and son was severed. With that I moved from a state of dependency to one of responsibility. I was on my way. For better or for worse I had no idea then but you will soon see.

The riots of 1958

"Human beings suffer. They torture one another. They get hurt and get hard. No poem or play or song can fully right a wrong inflicted and endured." "The Cure at Troy" by Seamus Heaney from "Hope and History" by Gerry Adams.

In 1958 the Tamils in Colombo were badly beaten up by the dominant community, the Sinhalese. There were killings, arson and looting. The looters behaved stereo typically. In the city mostly gangs roamed wild inflicting terrible depredations. They took everything that was worth taking and burned everything else. It was a Saturday around twelve O' clock. I was auditing Lewis Brown. We were advised to leave and get to our homes immediately. As I stepped on to McCallum road, the main road, a young man in sarong came charging towards me; no he was not going to beat me up as I feared. He picked up a log of wood that lay close and ran towards the rail station. We lived in Colombo which was predominantly Sinhalese. There was complete chaos, everyone felt unsafe and confused and anomie smothered the entire city. My father had seen a world war where the threat was from an external source and the enemy foreign. Their lives were shaped by the darkness of that war. Whereas here it was among people we have lived for generations. My parents decided to abandon Colombo and move to Jaffna which had a Tamil concentration.

One incident occurred of which I am proud of my parents. During the communal riots when the Tamils were looking desperately for ways to flee to Jaffna my friend, Noel Fernando who was a pilot in the air force came home and offered to fly my parents to Jaffna. No one else! Just the two of them he said. I conveyed this to my parents. My parents decided under no circumstances would they fly the coop when our Tamil neighbors were in a sorry plight. They stayed behind and left for Jaffna along with the other Tamils by special train.

My uncle and I

My parents had returned to Malaysia. My mother's younger brother was my guardian. A very conscientious man whose integrity was never ever been in question; a very bright person who did not go for higher studies for want of finances, and yet through dint of hard work rose to a very high position in the government service.

I had failed the university entrance examination. The only certificate I had was the General Certificate of Education (Advanced Level) with which I could do a five year course in Chartered Accountancy. I was given to understand this was a tough course. But if one passed the intermediate exam he is assured of a job with a decent salary.

I was keen on getting into a firm quick but uncle refused as he was anxious to have me admitted to one of the top two firms. When I pressed him one day he remarked, "I can get you into a firm today but I want you to join one of the big two and that may take a little time." Through his connections I did get into a prestigious British firm of Chartered Accountants where I served being a non-graduate a five year articles.

When I was at Jaffna College he would visit his parents in Jaffna. From the boarding I would spend part of my vacation with his parents, my grand- parents. During this brief visit he would test me on arithmetic. I would get most of it wrong. He would flog me as if administering a cure for a malady, to exorcise the demon of ignorance out of the system and introduce in its place a modicum of intelligence. On the last day before his departure to Colombo he would take me to the movies. I saw the movie "Spy Smasher" with him.

My days at Aquinas

It was called Aquinas University College preparing students for a University of London degree. I had failed the University of Ceylon entrance examination and continue to study I must. I enrolled here. Almost everyone attending this institution was a loser. Here were children of wealthy parents marking time to move into their family business.

Then there were those like me with no family business waiting in the wings, had failed the university entrance examination but must continue studying something for something. So long as I was studying my parents hadn't to worry about me and I too had a free rein.

One incident merits mentioning. My friend Rajah Praesoody (some will know him as a tennis star) Allan Pannambalana and I one afternoon drove up to a restaurant I think in Horton Place. Allan introduced me to the tasty, tingling gin and lime. Rajah had a Ford Anglia car. We "boarded" the car and took off. The next thing I remember a crowd peeping into the car. The car we were in summersaulted and then finally rested on all four. No one was even mildly injured. Proof that the car summersaulted was that there were road tar marks on the hood of the car.

At Aquinas I passed the Intermediate examination called the General Certificate of Education (Advanced Level) three out of the four subjects.

Me my mother and the movies

My mother was not given to outbursts of temper. Whenever she was emotionally disturbed she would pace up and down the corridor drawing inward saying nothing. My father was in Malaysia. My mother had come to Ceylon to look after my brother and me. At school the class was told we should see the movie *Pygmalion* by George Bernard Shaw which was later made into a movie, "My Fair Lady." I approached my mother and said to her I need to see this movie. My mother buttoned up. She became voiceless. She did not know what kind of movie it was. My mother like many other women in our community at that time was not English educated. The Tamil men and women who received an English education were mostly converts to Christianity. The church took them under its wings. So this was my mother's dilemma. Is it alright for young boys to see movies? Viewed from the perch of old age with two children and two grand- children I now realize she could not cope with the responsibility. There was no other male in the house with whom she could confer. I had to repeatedly tell her the movie was recommended by my teacher. It meant nothing to her. To her young children seeing movies was no good. Finally she yielded yet unsure whether she was doing the right thing. She gave me a rupee and ten cents and said this is it. Never ask to go for movies again. From now on I would save from my lunch money and go to the movies on the sly.

My father in tears

My father is not prone to demonstrations of grief. He would sit silently in a chair and brood. It is my mother who would give voice to their combined emotions. "Papa says this "and "Papa says that" would be the familiar preamble. But this day was different. My father had just returned after the cremation ceremonies of his youngest brother and was seated in the long tropical verandah in the Chankanai house in Jaffna.

I noticed he was deeply enwoven in the chain of his own thoughts within the silent embrace of his unspoken affection for his brother. I went to give him may be a cup of coffee and I detected large unwilling tears gathered in the corners of his eye lids and he seemed to be in great pain. That's the thing about pain. It demands to be felt. It must be felt. I was very proud of my father. No amount of words would have convinced me of his love for his youngest brother. It was clear he wanted to be left alone. I walked away. This made such an impression on my memory which nothing will ever efface.

How I came to do Accountancy

My parents were keen I should do some professional course. Talk of bringing down a 747 with a pistol. I was caught between Scylla and Charybdis, the devil and the deep blue sea; a blind man looking for a grey cat in a dark room.

There were only two professional courses I could have applied for with my Advanced Level certificate, Law and Accountancy. In law it would have to be the solicitor's called Proctors not the Attorneys course. Proctors at this time were second banana to Attorneys and not much respected. When asked to appear by the police at the traffic courts at Nahrenpita and as soon as you drive in proctors approach your car from all directions offering their services. Fancy me a beggar being a chooser.

It had to be therefore accountancy for which I had neither the stomach nor the ability. My parents contacted my uncle who had connections in the accounting world and I was second on the waiting list at the prestigious accounting firm, Turquand Youngs & Co. F.J Saga a Table Tennis player whom I knew well was in number one position.

While travelling by bus I see Saga in the same bus and he informs me he is withdrawing his name. I rang the bell, got off the bus went into A.B.C. café in Wellawatte and telephoned Turquand, Youngs and informed them that Saga was not interested. I was asked to report on Monday.

Accountants were so much in demand that with part qualification if one had served his articles in one of two leading accounting firms Turquand Youngs being one, Ford Rhodes and Thornton the other, with a convincing recommendation by a partner he could wind up with a good job.

That's how I got the job at Hunters with envious pay and perquisites.

In this inn there always was room

After the 1958 riots my parents left for our traditional home in the North and I became a lonely adult without a home or hearth.

I used to study in the evenings often late into the night with a friend who was living with his aunt. We were both serving articles with the same firm of Chartered Accountants, Turquand Youngs & Co. There were at this time living in this house which had (if I remember right) two large bed rooms, one small room, one bath room, dining, kitchen, pantry and a garage (Mr. V and Mrs. V) uncle and aunt of my friend, two sons, two daughters, my friend, his two brothers with Mr. V's father occupying the small room. There was a domestic help (for whom there was an outdoor toilet) added to the mix. When Mr. V's father died the little room was rented to me. It was Mr. and Mrs. V who accompanied me to visit my wife's home for the formal visit. My parents were not able to travel from distant Jaffna. Mr. and Mrs. V treated every one alike. There were no favorites in this house, not even their children who were very young. The food would be on the table the same food for all.

We all had to use one bath room and all of us had to leave the house for work or school before eight O'clock in the morning and this would be accomplished with Swiss watch precision. As soon as one finished his or her flash shower would call out, **"bath room free"** and the next person would jump in. Think of 4x100 meters Olympics relay. I have not known a single day when any one got late to work or school.

We continue to be close friends and I am deeply grateful to them for having given me board and lodging and friendship at a time I needed them most. It must have been difficult for Mr. and Mrs. V to carry on a normal life with the nephews around and what's worse a complete stranger prowling about the house.

As for me I was determined to be an ideal boarder exhibiting exemplary behavior. Remaining in my room studying most of the time during week-ends and during the week most of the time would be spent at the office. On occasions in the evenings my friend and I would go for walks to the beach. Whether I succeeded in being a non-interfering trouble-free boarder I do not know. I hope I was.

In a project such as this, while recounting old experiences certain events stand out. I would like to take this opportunity to treat this part of my narrative as a confession booth to atone for my complete lack of empathy, my gross insensitivity, not wink it away putting it down to callowness of youth. Incidents such as these will be written with feeling rather than reason. I believe it must be stated however uncomfortable it might make me. I feel now I could have made a larger financial contribution towards the family budget. They certainly could have used it. I regret this to this day.

I had got a job and was going to buy a car. So my motor scooter was up for sale. At this time my friend's brother who was living with us was on the look- out for a used scooter (called politely pre-owned in America) and I was approached as to whether I would drop a little on the price I was asking and I refused. How insensitive. We lived like one family. He is now a cardiologist enjoying a lucrative practice in the silk district of Los Angeles. As for me I am appalled by my insensitivity and selfishness.

Then there was this. There was a likelihood of Mr. V being allocated a government house and the whole family including the nephews could move in except me. This I overheard from my room. I felt very bad for until this moment I felt as being part of the family. I was disappointed. When I think back I admire Mr. V for this decision. He would have had to lie that I was part of the family to drag me in which he would not do under any circumstances.

I was seated in my room studying and I overheard this conversation. A relative asked Mr. V's daughter what kind of a person would you like to marry and bang came the answer, "some- one like my father." Need I say more?

No two persons we all know can agree on everything. Mr. and Mrs. must have had their disagreements but never disagreeable, harsh words did I hear being exchanged.

My first job

I had completed my five year articles (apprenticeship) during which period I should have become a qualified chartered accountant. The examination was split into two parts – Intermediate and Final. The final again has two parts. – Part 1 and Part 2. I passed the Intermediate. As for the Final, I passed Part 2 but kept failing Part 1. I was straining at the leash to get a job.

Every time I heard of a vacancy for an accountant in a large firm I would go up to the partner and tell him about it and his response to my disappointment was "that's not a good place for you." I was prepared to take it though. This went on for many months and I was beginning to get anxious and one day while I was auditing at Schweppes I get a call from my friend Sega that there was a vacancy in a well- known British company called Hunters. I stopped whatever I was doing, got permission from my supervisor, Thiagarajah and dashed off to see Hardstaff a partner. You cannot just walk into his office. You got to talk to Hardstaff's peon who will arrange the meeting. I was called in and when I mentioned to him the name of the company Hardstaff said "Hunters is a good firm, call Jesuant (his secretary)." With me out of the room he dictated a letter. I go up to Jesuant and say to him, "Mr. Jesuant could I have a copy please?" "Sorry the letter will be sealed. You send it with the application."

I was interviewed by the managing director Hockaday. White slacks, white long sleeves shirt tie and nervous I set out for Hunters. I was told my salary would be one thousand two hundred and fifty rupees a month, two bonuses a year, health insurance, company contribution of twenty five percent of my gross salary towards my retirement, goods from this hardware company at cost and more benefits. I was at this time earning one hundred and forty nine rupees and twenty five cents, seventy five cents having been deducted for union fees.

At the end of this sweet music, Bing Crosby crooning in my ears, a cartwheel moment, Hockaday, a chain smoker taps the cigarette ash into the tray and says, "May be you want to think about it." How should I react? If I agree to it immediately it would appear I was "cheap". On the other hand if I asked for time to think it over and in the interim he changed his mind then what happens? The offer was too good to miss. I said, "I'll take it." Without qualifying fully as a chartered accountant for temporary satisfaction I opted for a Faustian choice. I was later told many fully qualified accountants had applied for the job but Hardstaff's recommendation trumped all. I became later the first non-British chief accountant and secretary to the board of this company.

A few words about my first boss

A veteran of the Second World War, a Scotsman, ran the company like a platoon. "Yes sir", "No sir; a micro manager par excellence; first man at work and last to depart. His instructions were precise in brief typed notes- e-mails, what are they? Rifled through staff desks and left notes. The only time he took time off from smoking was to light up one more; believed in one on one dialogue with his executive staff; did not give a dang for staff meetings or consensus. You have your orders; you click your boots and keep marching lock-step if you know what's good for you. Under his watch the place ticked like a Swiss watch; valued loyalty and integrity to brilliance.

Neela and Deeran:
How I met your grandmother

I liked what I saw

My friend in whose aunt's house I was living got married and with his new bride left for England to continue his studies in accounting. I was like that single logo piece you do not know where to fit in. Like Robinson Crusoe without Friday, Don Quixote without Sancho Panza, Lone Ranger without Tonto. My friend and I were employed in different companies but in the evenings we would meet with mutual friends and do fun things. I was now lonely and you might say miserable. This did not go unnoticed by my friend's family with whom I was living.

They apparently decided it was their duty to now find a bride for me. There was this girl from a well- known and highly respected family in Colombo. She had passed the final degree with flying colors (remember I failed this exam twice in all subjects) distinguished herself at High School becoming the only Hindu girl ever to be made Head Girl of a leading Christian school in Colombo and was now teaching at the university.

My friend's cousin who knew this girl and I went in my car to the university and I was shown the girl who was talking to friends on the corridor. To sum it up if I may be permitted to turn on its head what Caesar said, "I came, I saw, I was conquered."

We were married and since that day on she has been the metronome of my life, my inner compass. My friends have never ceased needling me that the only time I had exhibited any kind of mental acuity is in the selection of my wife. My parents were pleased but had only one concern. This is a family that had been for generations vegetarians. My mother wanted to know how I notoriously a carnivore would fit in. I did not give it any serious thought at that time. My wife although completely at home with a vegetarian meal is omnivorous in her taste. A lively clear mind that can see what is relevant immediately, and around corners, a trait the children have happily inherited.

What continues to dazzle me to this day is the radiance of her mind. This scintillating quality, her astuteness had rescued the family from many catastrophes. At crucial moments she had by sheer force of her coruscating personality stepped in and we effectively used her as a cat's paw to pull the chestnuts out of the fire. There are numerous instances I can relate. My mother would often say one does not have to polish off a whole pot of rice in order to determine whether the rice is well cooked.

Suffice I hope it would be to give just two incidents.

The two incidents

Incident one

My wife, our daughter, our new born son and I were in Monrovia, Liberia. I was there to take on a new job. We had been put up at a modest hotel. I was nervous about this job and the country. I had no friends to lean on. My wife and I had many questions about this place. Where we could shop, the kind of people we are going to be meeting and many more imponderables that assaults a person taking residence for the first time. At this moment in- comes a gentleman and wife, *acquaintances* of mine in Freetown, Sierra Leone. I would have done anything to please them. I needed their friendship and help miserably badly. I would have gone any distance not to displease them. Just before departure the lady visitor said to my wife that it was unsafe to keep valuables in this hotel as robbery is rampant. She offered to take all her jewelry away for safekeeping. I was about to say "sure! Thank you" when my wife stepped in and said very courteously she would rather keep it.

Incident two

When we arrived in the U.S.A I was the only one who was authorized to work; a mortgage, settling down expenses, two cars and two children to see through college. So on one salary it was mighty hard to find the resources to send our son to college. Our daughter was already at college. And to college our son must go come hell or high water. Parents always want their children to do better than what they have achieved. I heard over the news they were entertaining applications for Reserve Officer Training Corps (R.O.T.C) and for those selected college tuition would be paid. I was seriously strapped for cash; strapped for cash in relation to my aspirations. I wanted my son to get a university degree. There was not going to be "ifs" and "buts" on this matter. I put this to my wife. I heard an emphatic no. If he had joined the R.O.T.C. we would have deprived him of the opportunity to make up his own mind whether or not to join and be drafted in times of war.

The other woman

The narrative, "I liked what I saw" should be juxtaposed with a previous meeting with another young lady. It is said memory is a neural muscle, and once you begin to stretch it, it grows to accommodate everything that has ever happened to you, often things you might prefer to forget. There was at this time what is traditionally termed a "marriage proposal" for me. It worked like this. Parents of unmarried girls get very anxious and want their daughters married pronto. Friends and relatives I believe scout around for eligible young men and arrange a meeting very often in a close relative's home. I was taken to this home in Jaffna by my very close friends, husband and wife. I have forgotten the details. All I remember is I was uneasy throughout this meeting. The relatives on my side were keen to know how I felt on my return from the "meeting". I did not give an answer. I went to Colombo and wrote to my parents in the negative. That was that. The girl's parents and relatives were convinced I had someone else in mind. Parents and relatives mindful of the girl's future prospects of marriage generally file it off this way.

My olden, golden days, my purple years in sports

The best table tennis match was against Chris Gunaratne in the Mackenzie House Finals. You may consider it as a Grand Slam in the world of Ceylon Table Tennis.

Chris was a very talented player, well liked with connections to the sports media and it was believed Chris would win effortlessly, a cinch. The organizers were so sure Chris would win that they decided what prizes should go to the champion and the runner-up. To Chris the presumed champion would go an expensive wrist watch, and for me the runner-up, perhaps they felt I needed good clothes gabardine material to make a full suit. The champion and runner-up would also get trophies.

A large crowd had come in early to get good seats. It was to be a best of five games. Whoever wins three becomes the champ. The match lasted a little over two hours. Chris won the first and I the second. Chris won the third and I the fourth - two all. It was now the final game and it went even all the way with me behind and catching up until it came to deuce which is twenty all. At this stage whoever gets a two point lead wins. I was a defensive player and Chris was hitting hard on both flanks – back hand and fore-hand. He now hit one very hard to my fore-hand and I had to go back as far as the wall to retrieve it. Since I was so far away from the table all he had to do was to drop the ball just over the net on my side of the table and I would have had to take a taxi to get there in time. This he attempted but failed. The ball fell on his side. The game was now twenty one – twenty in my favor. The next point went on for a while – Chris driving the ball hard and I retrieving all the time when finally he aced one to my back hand and I to everyone' surprise with my back to the wall retrieved it and the game was over. I was declared champ. An upset is how the papers announced it. Chris was disappointed and he needed the watch badly. I am glad I did the right thing. I gave the watch away to him. This win at the Mackenzie House championship placed me number two in Ceylon for that year. My neighbor and close friend for over sixty years Sri with whom I would walk along the beach to the club for practice every evening, who now lives one exit away accompanied me to and from the club witnessed the match.

On this day the world and life seemed complete, satisfactory and sufficient to me. My parents never watched any one of the many games I played.

On my grand- parents

I know very little about my grand- parents. My mother's father was an Ayurvedic physician (herbal medicine) and a small time farmer with a postage stamp size paddy field where he must have grown rice and some vegetable to feed his family. He was a good man. Never saw him in a foul mood or say harsh things. He could sing well. It is my belief he did not charge a fee for his medical service. Perhaps in kind like vegetables and rice by grateful patients. One thing to this date is a mystery; I have my take on this. When my mother was born my grand- father was sent to the Registrar of Births with instructions to register the name *Sivalakshmi*. It was not until many years later it came to light that she was registered as *Yogaratnam*, a boy's name. The family put it down to grandpa's forgetfulness. I think he liked the name *Yogaratnam* and so registered her as such. My mother did not wish to go by a boy's name. She truncated Yogaratnam to *Yogam* and came to be known as such.

I barely remember my grand- father on my father's side. I have a very faint recollection of my father's mother. She was taller than my grand –father who was abnormally short. It used to be said my grand – mother objected to his smoking cheroot and would take the tobacco leaf which he would roll to make his cheroot and place it on top of the cupboard where he could not reach. I have heard this repeated several times to the amusement of my relatives. I have no idea what he did for a living. The ladies of course tended to the home and the kids.

Threw discretion to the winds

My mother began pacing back and forth in the dining section of our apartment in Colombo. A sure sign she was deep in thought, worried, in great pain. Then she turned round and asked, "Why Chandra why are you leaving? You have such a fine job here." Yes. That's correct. I was sitting pretty on a well- paying job, the kind you check-in at nine and check-out at five and no headaches to follow you home. A charming wife who gave mathematics tuition at home during the day, the last student would be dismissed before I arrived from work and a daughter, delightful little girl of one and eleven months.

So what was my response? "Didn't papa leave his parents and go too." That killed all conversation on the subject in the crib.

There is a period near the beginning of every person's life when he has little to cling to except his dream and good health and in my case the predilection to travel perhaps imprinted in my genes it had become a biological necessity that I should travel and with complete disregard to a mother's feelings.

There was a change in government about this time. The new government was socialist, left leaning and in a hurry to nationalize (take over) large companies. There was a joke doing the rounds at this time. Went like this. A man in a line doing pee in a public Mens' was seen making a huge show of hiding his "manliness." The neighbor intrigued by his peculiar behavior asked why he was making such a big fuss over what everyone in line had. The man it is said then replied, "Don't you know the government is nationalizing anything that's big."

My accountant friends were leaving in droves accepting job offers in Nigeria and Zambia in Africa. I wanted to leave too. I was rearing to go. I had a preexisting condition which they did not. They were fully qualified chartered accountants whereas I was what used to be mockingly referred to "a half qualified accountant" having not completed all parts of the Final. My applications were either ignored or met with polite rejections.

Then it came to pass.

My wife and I routinely on Friday nights after dinner, having tucked our daughter into bed and leaving her in the care of a domestic help would go to our friend's house (the same friend who accompanied me to the table tennis match) and chin-wag till late into the night. My friend's father – in – law at this time a distinguished jurist was Chief Justice in Sierra Leone. A new corporation the first of its kind with private companies and the government contributing towards the equity was formed and an accountant preferably one from outside the country was urgently needed. The Board of Directors approached my friend's father-in law to find one from Ceylon.

My application was accepted. I was informed to await the tickets. Weeks went by and there was no sign of tickets. I would from Hunters walk up to British Airways and inquire only to be told "Sorry nothing for you". I had to give notice of ceasing employment in order that I can take off as soon as the tickets arrived. And so once more faithful to my nature I gambled. Without the tickets in hand I handed to the Acting Managing Director a letter informing him I would be leaving employment by a certain date. He took the letter and placed it in the top right hand drawer of his desk and said to me "See me when you get your tickets."

A few days later British Airways called to say the tickets had arrived. When I visited the Acting Managing Director to give him the news and wish him Good Bye he opened the drawer took my letter giving notice and said, "I have not submitted it to the board. I was waiting to make sure you got your tickets. Now I will."

Thus dear friends blessed with the optimism of youth, the tiger juices flowing, spurred by giddy ambition, propelled by a romantic desire to see the world, intoxicated by the possibilities of a new beginning, egged on by the hope of a better life elsewhere with nothing more than adrenaline for assurance, without pausing to ponder how I was going to manage my life, when children become chattel, just another piece of luggage you must have your eye on, staking all on a single moment, on a fleeting whim, a fancy, risking everything on one throw at the spinning wheel, not realizing the cosmic dice once rolled cannot be picked up again, I with my wife Siva and infant daughter, Gaitri set out for Sierra Leone. We did not know where on earth Sierra Leone was. We looked up the Atlas.

This was in the break of dawn of the nineteen seventies. An odyssey on roller skates had been set in motion.

On my parents

I was not an abused child like Michael Jackson. I did not grow up in a dysfunctional home like that of Frank McCourt or born into a family without a father like Jean Paul Satre.

No dear readers I had loving parents whose only concern was to bring my brother and me up as descent human beings and give us an education. Yes when it came to education nothing would be spared. Everything else was back-burner. There was a time while in Ceylon I was keen to go to England to do my accountancy examinations signs of early symptoms of the fever to travel abroad, a ploy no doubt to see the world. My parents did not have the money but mother was willing to part with her jewelry to raise the money. Should I get late to return home after table tennis practice at the club, I should be home by six, I could see from a distance my mother walking restlessly up and down the street. No sooner she had spotted me she would dash into the house and be seated in the chair as if unconcerned. I would fall asleep at the dining table studying. My mother to help keep me stay awake would sit with me and read a magazine. A mother is a fulcrum to our lives. If we consider a family as a wheel the mother is the hub.

When I visited my parents in Jaffna and would walk at the end of the visit to the front gate to get into the taxi my father every time would, leaving my mother in the front verandah come running up to me and whisper, "Ammah worries about you. Please write to her. Never mind me."

My father like many others of his time was the sole bread winner believing steadfastly the measure of a man is how well he provides for his family and like so many of her peers my mother remained at home and honed her domestic skills, tending to the welfare of her children. Whatever their limitations and frailties, those who raised me loved me in the best way they knew how. Of that I am certain.

I was not with my parents when they passed away. There was at that time a civil war raging in Ceylon. Even the cable informing me of their deaths reached me days after the event. I don't cultivate guilt – that's greasy self-indulgence. I wish I could redeem the loss, not stew in the bitter juice of memory, if I can.

When parents die they leave holes in our hearts and we can find nothing to plug it with. I would like to end with a quote from E.M.Forster:

"A wonderful physical tie binds the parents to the children. And by some strange irony it does not bind us children to our parents. For if it did, if we could answer their love *not with gratitude* but with equal love, life would lose much of its pathos and much of its squalor and we might be wonderfully happy."

Letter to our grand-daughter

Sweet Neela

When you were in Connecticut the last time, I saw you looking at Appi's eagle - scout paraphernalia with a mixture of wonderment and joy. I am therefore certain you will want to know the drama and excitement that surrounded your Appi's birth. The cautionary words you will hear me repeat time and again are in the title, "This much I remember and this is how I remember it."

Amama, Apapa and Gaitri Mami a tiny girl then were at this time living in Freetown, Sierra Leone. A beautiful house along the sea you could hear the sound of the waves kindly lashing against the wall that separated the sea and the house. Ships go so close to the house you could see the sailors doing work on deck.

Amama was expecting Appi. A Sierra Leonean gynecologist trained in Scotland was treating her. Then one day Amama was told that problems might very likely occur because of what is called the Rhesus factor. You could read more about this. The good doctor advised that it would be a smart move to have the baby in London. Sanath Mama was contacted and he advised that Amama should proceed to London as it would be too expensive in the United States. Like in all matters the question of cost came into the equation. We contacted my cousin Manis, a gynecologist in London on this matter. She informed us to be prepared for at least three thousand pounds sterling, may be more. We had at this time at the Barclays Bank in London may be a little over three thousand pounds. Amama and I discussed its ramifications and in a short time decided to go for it, once again threw caution to the winds. As you can see it was a good investment. Pon Party and Parta were fortunately living in London and so Amama was dispatched there. She would travel with Gaitri by bus to the hospital and the good people she said would kindly offer her a seat. Fortuitously the doctor treating Amama was Dr. Kaineki a world renowned Harley Street authority on Rhesus factor.

As feared Appi was born jaundiced and had to be given several blood transfusions. So you see your Appi has plenty of British blood in him. When I came to London to see Appi I was not allowed inside the room. I had to see Appi through a glass partition for fear of infection.

Now the cost: Amama was not discharged as the hospital wanted to make certain she could nurse Appi to health. Amama began to fear the longer she stayed bigger would be the bill. When she made this known to the nurse she replied your son having been born in Britain takes on British citizenship immediately and all British citizens get free medical attention. Further she said, "I am not going to be announcing you are a visitor." The only expense was the doctor's fee which did not amount to much. Apapa and Amama made a special visit to the hospital and presented the nurses with chocolates which they accepted reluctantly because as they said we need not have gone through all that expense. The name Girisha was given by a sweet aunt of Amama.

Girisha: Means lord of the mountain, the name of the Hindu god Shiva whose sacred abode is in the Himalayas.

Letter to our grand-son

Sweet Deeran

Your Ammi soon after birth gave us quite a run. She was born in a private nursing home in Colombo. Viji Mami was also expecting at this time was present during Ammi's birth. All went well. Then a nurse who was tending on Ammi mentioned to Amama that she observed Ammi had turned blue. All panic broke loose. Amama and Apapa were very worried because the nurse said that it is a symptom of what is called "a hole in the heart."

Amama pulled out Sanath mama's connections – the A.K 47s. Drs. Priyani Zoysa, Nanayakara, Karunyan. They made frequent visits to the nursing home to check on Ammi. The nursing home authorities were thoroughly impressed by the celebrity doctors visiting the nursing home. It was decided Ammi should be X-rayed. Dr. Karunyan accompanied us to the place where your Ammi was x-rayed. As the nursing home did not have an X-ray machine Ammi was taken to a private institution in Borella.

As you can see Deeran Your Ammi is doing more than fine.

Gaitri: A variant of Gayatri mantra, the foremost mantra in Hinduism a mantra that inspires wisdom.

Permission to stay in the U.S. denied

If I am to list the times I felt very scared this would figure very prominently, high close to the summit. I remember so well. I was working at Narrotam Systems. The time was around four O'clock, a bright sunny day. My desk faced the window. I like it that way.

The telephone rang and I listened. The one on the other end did not even have to introduce himself. Our voices were familiar to the other. We have spoken so many times face to face and by telephone. "Chandraraj:" the caller growled. From the tone I knew it is bad news. "You have to see me right-away." It was my attorney Mr. Cohen. I go immediately to my supervisor and say to him that my attorney wants me over on an urgent matter. Take the # 6 Down Town to Canal Street walk through China Town and to Cohen's office on Broadway. I could get there blind-folded.

I was expected. As soon as I sat opposite Cohen he handed me a printed note from Immigration. "It will be necessary for you to depart from the United States not later than September 10, 1990." I felt dizzy. I went blank. "How can I leave like that? I own a house, two cars, my wife and two children" Observing me closely he said after a while, "It does not make any difference" Cohen "assures" me. "There could be one way out. Here is an application form for political asylum. Fill it now and give it to me. I could not do it. I felt the juices squeezed out of me. I was far too upset. Cohen noticing this and feeling sorry for me brings his chair round and sitting beside me filled the form in his own hand writing. "Many people apply for political asylum as a dodge. I do not know how yours will be treated" Cohen says.

The return journey from Grand Central to Bridgeport station where my car was parked was unbearable torture. I cried internally – deep hemorrhagic in tears. The most difficult thing for me to ever do is to come home and proffer bad news affecting the whole family. From now on I feel insecure and hesitant in whatever I undertook. I envied those who did not have this sword of Damocles hanging over their heads.

I attended the immigration hearings (in the waiting room I noticed several Chinese in chains) with Cohen in attendance. He said I could go alone but should he accompany me it would cost one hundred and fifty dollars. I agreed on the fee. Whether this made a difference or not I do not know, the immigration official and Cohen were buddies. I received a letter stating my wife and I could call at the Federal Building in the city to collect our work visas. My wife, our son and I went. My wife and I received the work permit. At the office while the preliminaries were being worked out my wife, always alert, asked the officer whether our son too could get a work permit. The lady said yes he can and he too obtained one. Through- out this process my wife's and my spirits were very low. But our son kept us going by his good humor. To reward him we asked him where he would like to have lunch and pat came the reply, "Hard Rock Café." And Hard Rock Café it was.

Dreams

"If you do not have a dream how you gonna have a dream come true." So goes the song. But my experience has been some dreams come true and some turn out just pipe dreams.

My father's bosses were British and it so happened mine too were most of the time. In Malaysia my teachers were British and later in Colombo my bosses too were. The British always were aloof and never mixed with the indigenous population. They by their demeanor and conduct demanded respect and I like so many of my compatriots gave it to them in spades.

I remember very well my first day at the accounting firm, where I served my articles (apprenticeship) which was wholly British owned at that time. I was seated cross-legged at the long desk occupied by juniors. The gentleman, a Ceylonese who helped me get a place at this firm came up tapped my shoulder and said to me "Thamby (Son) put your leg down." I promptly did so. I got the message that it was a sign of disrespect to the white partners to be seated thus. Kind of cocky eh! I saw all around me elderly senior Ceylonese executives spring to attention when a partner came over to speak to them. The white partners were a class by themselves. There was holy respect for them. The Ceylonese I noticed who returned from England after qualifying as chartered accountants too behaved like the British partners. They were a tribe apart from the rest. Always talking about the English weather, British politics and reading the London Times in the elevator so as to politely ignore the rest of us. They even talked differently which was to my liking. England certainly changes people. They become sophisticated and polished. Plenty of "Please"; "Thank you"; "No Thank You and "Pardon me"

I now join Hunters as accountant where the Directors, Managing Director and Chairman of the Board are all British. They behave the same way as their compatriots in the accounting firm. Very reserved and upper crust I must say. When the managing director or chairman should come to my room I stand up instantly as if there are springs on the soles of my shoes. There would be just one party for the whole year and that would be just before Christmas. To this party the Ceylonese executives would be invited. The talking would be all done by the white folks, the rest of us looking up in silent admiration. Every now and then the managing director or chairman could be heard saying "This is the way we do it in the U.K." Everything was superlative over there I was convinced

I want to visit England. I want to see this place where everything is right. Like Dick Whittington's London where the streets were paved with gold. Everything we bought was "Made in England." If not we would not buy it. The two cars I owned were Wolseley 1300 and Hillman Minx – made in England.

So when the tickets came for me, my wife and daughter to fly to Sierra Leone to take on the job I requested British Airways to route the journey through London and it was granted after obtaining approval from my employer. I was excited beyond speech. My wife's brother and family were living in Newcastle, England. We got to see him. Some- one has to meet us at the airport. I would not know what to do if there was no one to receive us. This is my first overseas trip. The Ceylon Exchange Control allowed me just ten pounds sterling. I wrote to my cousin in London and five of my friends separately giving flight details.

My brother in law cautioned me England will be cold in December and I should procure an overcoat. Yes that would be grand, me in an overcoat, just like in the movies (why no gloves?) just like Gregory Peck in "The man in the grey flannel suit" The transformation was about to begin. I would have no use for this overcoat in Sierra Leone. I made inquiries and was informed I could get a used (sorry 'pre owned') one from "Sellamuttus" in the Pettah. When I called at the shop I was taken to a room where there was a mountain of overcoats piled one over the other and was invited to choose any one. One price! These were returns by returning Ceylonese.

Arrival in London

Throughout the flight the ten pounds remained untouched. Just in case no one is there to receive us. The plane was now approaching London Heathrow airport and we were informed that we will be landing in half an hour. I could not contain my excitement. I kept looking out through the window. The lights were brilliant. They were sparkling. It was plain beautiful. Funny! All at once I find myself right in immigration. I did not have to walk the tarmac. How come? There were other things to think about. I wear my over coat and pleased the way everything worked out so far I proudly dipped my hands like in the movies into my coat pockets for no reason. I felt some stuff in there. When I checked they were cigarette butts. Now at the terminal I keep looking out for my friends. I counted five of them there. The five I wrote to. And they knew each other. When each person asked the other who was expected every one of them said Chandraraj. It was getting late. While I was greeting my friends at the terminal very briefly my cousin had loaded her mini minor car with our bags and had started the car. Quickly waving good bye to my friends who had come to receive me spending barely five minutes with them we were off. All night I kept looking at the street from my bed, say it softly like a prayer, "This ees London."

Opening my first bank account in London

I had done some tax work for my Hunters boss and he said he would like to give me one hundred pounds sterling. He wanted to know where he should send it. I gave my brother- in - law's address in the United Kingdom. On arrival in London I was eager to open a bank account as I would be sending all my savings here from Sierra Leone. My cousin Manis requested her colleague to take me to Barclays at Balham and get the job done. In Ceylon opening an account at the bank is a prolonged sentence with witnesses and several guarantors. On arrival at the bank Manis's friend points to a window and carries on with whatever she has to do. I am far from happy. How do I handle this all by myself singlehanded? I nervously approached the window and said in the best English I could command that I wish to open an account and proffered the ten pounds sterling I had brought with me from Ceylon untouched throughout the journey and assured the officer he could expect a hundred pounds very soon. He pushes a 4x6 card and asked me to fill it. One side only. Full name and address to which bank statement should be sent and sign. I did so and waited for the inquisition all the while looking at Manis's friend to come over. I was still waiting with a line forming behind me and the officer says, "You may go. We will mail you the receipt for the deposit."

Hardstaff, Gordon and Hockaday were right. Everything is super in England.

Thereafter we leave by train for Newcastle and my brother-in-law was at the station to receive us.

On sighting me his first words of greetings were "Parana coat" (old coat). Old coat may be but I felt like Cary Grant in "An Affair to remember."

The little dreams that came true

When I was living in my friend's aunt's house while a student I recall reading Groucho Marx's "A night in Casablanca." It was hilarious. And I thought to myself how wonderful it would be to see Casablanca. Well on one of our vacation trips from Sierra Leone to London by British Caledonian Airways the aircraft developed engine trouble and we had to stay overnight in Casablanca. In the night after tasting the best croissants ever we walked over to the bazar close to the hotel. I fancied a leather jacket going cheap – no returns. More cigarette butts in the pockets!

I remember reading in the Ceylon Daily News that there was tension in Skokey, U.S.A. The skinheads were going to march in protest against the Jews. I have no idea what the skinheads were angry about. I was certain there would be bloodshed and so waited for the day of the march. Permit had been obtained from the police by the skinheads to march. The judge allowed it. The world was watching. On the day of the march it was orderly and no heads were broken. "Man" I said to myself it must be great to live in Skokey. Great to live in a country where the minorities get police protection. I did not feel secure in Colombo. I wish I could visit this Skokey some- day. My son and family now live in Wilmette and when we visit them it's to Skokey we drive to get our pizza.

Some dreams turn out pipe dreams

Even though I was what derisively described "a half qualified accountant" I had accumulated a great deal of experience working in third world countries holding responsible positions. I was always dreaming of a United Nations job. It carried great prestige and excellent pay with envious benefits. What is also attractive about a" U.N. Job" is we seldom hear of anyone being fired for incompetence. How about that? I now know sometimes one's ability can fall short of his aspirations. I was Accountant General in Sierra Leone with good connections. I knew the Minister of Finance, The Financial Secretary, The Development Secretary and many other high muckety-mucks personally. I was on intimate terms with them. Talk of right place and right time.

I approached all the pooh-bahs and suggested to them to have the position of Accountant General be funded by the United Nations. They gave the fullest support and wrote to the United Nations representative in Sierra Leone. The representative viewed it favorably. I received a draft contract. Then I do not know what happened. Everything came to a stand- still and the rep was not talking. Even to the top government officials. They call it radio silence don't they?

The Minister of Development suggested I should apply to the British Commonwealth office as they need accountants with third world experience. I applied and one day there came an offer for a six-month tour with possibility of extension in the Dominican Republic. At this time I already had obtained a work visa in the United States. I was not going to throw away the chance of coming to the United States and yet it was difficult to sniff at an international position I had long sought. I kept asking for more and more time until one day I received a letter that the position had been withdrawn.

I was at this time living in Shelton. I was about to run down the stairs and head for the garage. The bed room 'phone rang. I had half a mind to ignore it but that inner voice said "take it." My friend Ferry from the I.M.F says to me to send him my resume. There is a job for you with the I.M.F. in Eritrea. I applied even though my heart was not in it as my wife could not accompany me. An Englishman, an Italian American (I cannot recall their names) and my friend of Turkish- Iranian descent arrived in Asmara, the capital of Eritrea after a two day delay in Frankfurt, Germany due to a snow storm.

Two incidents come to mind about Frankfurt, Germany.

Rest of the team went through immigration smoothly. Minutes before I was to step in I could see two immigration officials seated side by side whisper to each other and then a belittling smirk on their faces. They had already profiled me. Third world like egg was all over my face. They had decided that my papers will have flaws; sneak into the country with false documents, the usual routine.

They were ginned up to have some fun. The immigration official stretched out his hand and I gave the papers to him. He looked very hard. Turned it over and over. The papers confirmed that I have been approved for United States citizenship and therefore had all the privileges of a U.S. citizen.

All aircrafts were grounded due to heavy snow and we were booked at the airport hotel. I remember walking restlessly at the airport, hoping we can take off soon. I was repeatedly informed we will be delayed for a while. At this time I saw a large aircraft taxying for a take -off. I run up to an official and ask how come that aircraft is allowed to depart. That he says is the prince of Saudi Arabia. It's his private jet.

My experience with African countries is when you go as an invitee of the government all immigration and customs formalities are waived. You are taken direct to the visitors' lounge and then to the hotel with baggage cleared unopened.

At the Treasury where we reported for work while other members of the team went off to meet departmental heads Ferry and I met with a high official. He also acted as our point man. An affable gentleman who will say "sure, sure" for anything you say to him. I attended a meeting with the head of the Treasury and other officials. At the end of the meeting I was told I should plan to return in two weeks. I wanted a month. I also met the I.M.F. representative in Asmara. The only question I asked him was about health facilities and was told I will be flown out, very likely to Germany. *It is pertinent to mention here during our entire stay in Africa we had no health insurance coverage.*

My thoughts were what would be the position if I am not in a condition to be flown out. It was pretty obvious the country economically was in a parlous state. I remember during a break from a joint meeting with the officials I had to urgently do a pee. I entered the ill lit room and there it was a hole in the ground with stuff all over. I shot it down with eyes closed. As I got out the Englishman who was waiting for my opinion wanted to know how it was out there. I said, "I wouldn't go there again." It must have been a "gota go" situation for him and so he went.

We were invited to a dinner at a restaurant with very bad lighting. Perhaps they were conserving energy. I observed our hosts were very busy talking in whispers moving from group to group. We were completely ignored. Two days after we departed fighting broke out between Eretria and Ethiopia and all foreign personnel were flown out. On the night of the dinner Eritreans were being told by their leader to prepare for war.

I was anxious to bring home a souvenir something, anything from Eritrea. I walked back and forth the streets adjacent to the hotel and could not find any. The shops were bare, the shelves empty. Signs of depression and poverty everywhere and mind you we are talking about the capital, Asmara. Since we were not permitted to take pictures I had not taken my camera. All I have to show that I had been to Eritrea is the stamped immigration documents.

Thus my dream to work for a United Nations agency ended up in a pipe dream.

My first job in Liberia

This was in the late nineteen seventies. I was offered employment in Liberia with a motor firm on a decent salary. And so the whole family, now wife, daughter and son moved to Monrovia, the capital of Liberia. Monrovia was named after President Monroe of the United States.

On my arrival a company official took mine and my family's passport for immigration and customs purposes. Thereafter I never saw the passports. Later I learned this is how they controlled the movement of expatriates working for them. The company was owned by Lebanese nationals. They were a powerful force in Liberia. They owned practically all the major businesses. High and low government officials were well provided for and so the owners had a free run. Where working hours were concerned the starting time alone was fixed. Thereafter you had to keep working until the General Manager was ready to go home very often around eleven O'clock at night. On Saturdays a "big concession"; we could start at ten in the morning and close shop around four in the evening. The General Manager would keep his office door open and he could see the staff at work. My predecessor accountant was an Indian and I was told this story. He was newly married and was living with his wife. He could no longer take this severe regimen and so one day around eleven O'clock in the night he decided to leave. The routine is you wait for the General Manager to say, "lets- go" and then begin locking up the place. As he was walking away around eleven O'clock the General Manager called out "Where do you think you are going?" and he replied I am going home to bring my bed." He did not show up the next day.

By my demeanor it was clear to the General Manager and President that I was not going to fit in. I was called in after a few months of working and fired. There was no discussion. No talk about my passports. It was a very difficult time for me. I remember one day while our son was under the care of our good friend Mrs. Chels (we would call her auntie Chels) my wife, our daughter and I without saying a word were walking along the corridors of an office complex on Broad Street. My wife's and my heart were heavy with fear. Loaded like rifles about to go off. We kept asking in our heads where do we go from here? What do we do? I had dynamited the bridge before crossing it. Then suddenly our daughter began to whimper. She sensed the tension the parents were experiencing. I had to find a job in order to stay on and soon.

About my boss:

His family was living outside the country. Until four in the evening he is out of the office ostensibly at the bank or with the lawyers. Comes in at four, opens the mail and begins to dish out assignments with "stickies" marked "URGENT", "V. URGENT", "VV URGENT" "IMPT", V. IMPT". All one has to do is to remove the stickies and they cease to be "V.V. URGENT" and "V. IMPT" He would insist that staff at all levels should stay on until he leaves. Did I hear someone ask Labor laws? You are kidding aren't you?

My second job in Liberia

Our two Ceylonese friends, Chels and Maha for whom my book on humor was dedicated "fixed me up" as controller at the National Housing Authority (the first non -Liberian to hold that position), a government agency that was constructing homes for middle income families.

This is worth mentioning. The routine is the driver would pick up our daughter (she was in kindergarten class) at noon from school, take her home and then come for me. On this day the driver did not come to work and so I had to pick up our daughter at twelve O'clock. There was an important heads of departments meeting with the president of the Housing Authority. It was attended by all the architects and me the controller. For no reason whatsoever I glanced at my watch. It was one O'clock. "Good grief man." I should have picked up our daughter at twelve. I was sweating not knowing what may have taken place. Got excused from the meeting, jump into the car and made a dash for the school. As I approached the entrance I could see her seated on the steps of the school all alone with her little lunch box at her side. As she saw the car she came up to it opened the door and got into it. Not a squeak.

About my boss

Five foot two with a twelve foot personality he was alumni of Sorbonne University and the London School of Economics. Fluent in English and French he could dictate reports in either one. He had a full grasp of the corporation's many projects and had in view at all times the big picture, the grand scheme of things. He knew where he wanted to take the corporation and he enlisted the cooperation of his staff to go along with him on the journey. He put into practice precisely what Alan Kay believed: "The best way to predict the future is to invent it."

My third job in Liberia

I was able to handle the National Housing job comfortably but the pay was far from adequate even with my wife teaching. We occupied a little apartment in "down town condition." Chels and Maha our dear friends were aware of this. Our families would have dinner Friday nights in Chels's house and Saturday lunch at Maha's. There was a vacancy at a plumbing company that had World Bank contracts and the company was in search for an accountant. With the recommendation of Chels I eased into this job.

The Juju Man

While living in Jaffna in Sri Lanka I have heard of what is called "sooniams" where, by "magical powers" through incantations a priest-like man can detect lost property and even describe the thief. I have never witnessed one.

What I describe below I actually witnessed.

I reported this in my blog http://backhandflick.blogspot. com in May 2007 under the caption "I was present when it all happened" and I repeat verbatim.

It happened over quarter century ago. Not many events remain intact within the folders of my fading memory but this continues to be cuddled in my cranium.

It happened in Monrovia in the West African state, Liberia. Liberia is the only state in all of Africa that was not colonized by a foreign power. Monrovia, the capital was named after James Monroe, the fifth president of the United States. The capital Monrovia at this time had a population of approximately one hundred and fifty thousand inhabitants.

It is believed that the carrion complexion and kinky hair of the Negroid strain is recessive. So too I have found from all my peripatetic peregrinations from coast to coast and across continents that they are a people who exult in the act of sharing what little they possess with as many as they can find without a tincture of regret or remorse.

I was employed as controller of a construction company in Monrovia, engaged in World Bank projects. The staff comprised of Italians, Ghanaians, Nigerians, Sierra Leoneans, and of every tribe in Liberia. The president of the company, a master plumber was trained in the United States. A man of about five foot four was built like a fire hydrant. He was one who believed he should first treat himself to the very best. Caviar, champagne and the Concord. Nothing less. Although he had a proclivity for pampering himself with the first take, he was of generous and forgiving temperament.

At a certain point of time during my sojourn with the company strange things began to happen. Every Monday morning when we reported for work, items of small value were found to be missing. The value of items began getting bigger and bigger as the Mondays rolled by. From pocket calculators to heavy adding machines. It now reached a point when it became a guessing game as to what would be missing. Men and women would discuss the robbery in whispers in corners. There were no signs ever of a break-in. There was no need of a Sherlock Holmes. "Elementary Doctor Watson" It was an inside job. These facts set in motion a torrent of indictments by innuendo turning the atmosphere at work noxious and inter staff relationship divisive and debilitating. I felt I was left out of the lasso of suspects only because I, a foreigner, would not wager, put in jeopardy a lucrative contract of employment.

It was a Saturday. It was around eleven thirty in the morning. The closing time was twelve noon. I observed men and women running down the stairs making a loud noise. I followed the sound and found myself in the yard adjoining the main office. A circle had been formed. In the center, squatted, was a man, unkempt, gaunt, with a face resembling a battle axe, dressed in African garb on which time had left her grisly marks projecting that supercilious, imperious comportment of a Liberian cop. He had a rusty basin with yellow liquid, a machete and some leaves. On inquiry I was informed he was a Juju man and had been sent for by the president. His job was to identify the thief. The president too was present.

The Juju man proceeded to call those present to come one by one and take the test. He would request the participant to hold one end while he held the other end of the machete. He placed some leaves on the machete and sprinkled the yellow liquid from the basin. The tested was then asked to loosen the grip on the machete and withdraw his hand. A guilty person would not be able to let go of the machete we were told. Everyone present passed the test. I was not called. I teetered towards volunteering for the experience but backed off. I had no faith in this addled arcane art of detection and feared of being implicated.

What bewildered me more was in the circle of participants were members of the staff who were sophisticated, skilled professionals educated and trained in the United States, very Western in their ways in conduct and bearing who were readily submitting themselves to the dictates of a Juju man and unquestioningly awaiting the outcome.

At this point someone in the circle asked, "Where is Alfred?" He is in the office working on the payroll came the reply. "Send for him" the president ordered. Alfred Koroma (name given by me) a Sierra Leonean was always the first to arrive and last to leave the office. Reticent, intractable, always with a tortured expression he kept mostly to himself. He was for the most part deferential and distant in his dealing with his conferees. Alfred arrived. He had that perplexed "What is this all about?" look. He was asked to submit to the now familiar routine.

Alfred held the machete at one end and the Juju man held the other. Leaves were placed and the yellow liquid sprinkled as before. The juju man now asked Alfred Koroma to loosen his grip on the machete and remove his hand. He could not. He tried very hard. A gasp escaped from the crowd and then then was total silence.

The Juju man lapsed into an incantation lasting about a minute or two at the end of which Alfred was able to let go of the machete. Alfred got testy. He remonstrated that the whole exercise was a farce and should not be relied upon. The Juju man with unflappable demeanor asked Alfred "Are you challenging me?" Alfred hesitated and then with a hang-dog expression replied between clenched teeth "NO" and made a dash for his cubicle faster than a discharged bullet. It is believed that had Alfred challenged the veracity of this test the Juju man could cast a spell and some harm would come to him before sun set.

The president was a witness to all this. He returned to his office, his head bowed with that anguish that takes hold of a jockey when agonizing whether or not to shoot his injured horse. He said nary a word. Alfred was his favorite. His pride his pick of the litter.

Alfred Koroma was not fired. He was not called upon to pay for the stolen property. He was not admonished. The robberies stopped and Mondays resumed their uneventful monotony once more.

As some of us trundle forward in the twilight time of our lives we begin to live our lives backwards which bring to mind these timeless caressing and comforting words of Wordsworth.

"For oft when on my couch I lie in vacant or in pensive mood they (memories) flash upon that inward eye which is the bliss of solitude."

About my boss

"You have to treat yourself to the best there is. No one else will do it for you." was the guiding principle of his life. And so he flew by "Concord" to look up his girl friend in New Jersey for a week-end, drank the best scotch, changed his air conditioned Ford pick up every two years, customized for his convenience and personally supervised by him in the United States. A fire hydrant comes to mind when you first set eyes on him.

We leave Liberia chop- chop

And then it happened. I was during this period you can say religious. Religious fervor (or is it fever?) visits me now and then like the flu. It was around five in the morning and I was in the prayer room. I heard pop-pop sounds like fire crackers. It went on for a long time. The army led by master sergeant Samuel K. Doe had successfully carried out a coup. We now heard over the radio and television that president Tolbert had been assassinated by his own body guard Master Sergeant Samuel K. Doe. Ministers were hauled out of their homes and publicly executed. I saw our neighbor the minister of agriculture being taken away. Looting was rampant. Our domestic help in the evenings would change into comfortable clothes and sneakers and set out to loot. Cars of expatriates were stopped by soldiers and taken away. I knew they would come for my company-owned car. It was now around eight in the morning. I went out and waited in the verandah. As expected a jeep with soldiers arrived at our house and a soldier jumped out of the car, came up to me and demanded the keys to my car. I informed him that the car was not mine. It belonged to the company owned by a Liberian. The answer I got - a few gun shots fired in the air. I gave them the keys, in the bunch was a Sierra Leone diamond given to me as a present. I asked whether I could take my books from the car. They agreed.

The car was later abandoned. When gas was used-up the soldiers would abandon the car and commandeer one more. Even now the thought of those days chills my heart.

We practically gave away all our belongings and returned to Ceylon.

Kan Kam appears to me

This experience bothers me a lot. My assistant at the plumbing company was a Ghanaian. Extremely good fellow. Knew not even a vague hint of double entry book keeping; wherever I went on official business he would accompany me. He would pump gas for the car and gladly anything else I wanted him to do. He was living alone. His family lived in Ghana. He would visit Ghana once a year and with every visit his wife became pregnant. He had several children. He was kind to children. He would tell me very often, "Mr. Raj your son would turn out to be a smart guy." I know he was very fond of me.

I was informed one night that he had died of a heart attack. I went to his home where many from Ghana had gathered. The body was in the morgue. We had visitors from Freetown, Sierra Leone and so that night I slept on the sofa in the living room. In the middle of the night I felt Kan Kam tugging at my heart and imploring pathetically to come along with him. I had to wrestle to get rid of him. This went on what appeared to me for a long time. He finally left me alone.

In Sierra Leone: (West Africa)

My first job in Sierra Leone

This was in the early nineteen seventies

The National Trading Company:

The National Trading Company (N.T.C.) was unique in the sense it was a joint partnership of Government and the private sector, the first of the kind. It had the sole monopoly over the importation of basic items of food consumed everyday by Sierra Leoneans such as onions, tomato paste, sugar, evaporated milk, coffee and the like. I was appointed Senior Accountant. I am told initially my designation was to be Accountant and my Sierra Leonean deputy to be called Assistant Accountant. He did not like the title and so he was called Accountant and I, Senior Accountant. I later learnt that they were wary about calling me Chief Accountant, just in case I demanded a bigger pay.

I recall on the ferry, we have to go by ferry from Lungi airport to the mainland, I was asked by my assistant Tejan who came to receive me with Amara whether I had attended any company board meeting. I replied I was

Company Secretary/Chief Accountant of a fairly large company. I did not understand why the question was asked.

We were booked at the Brookfield's Hotel and in the evening the General Manager, John Solomon and a lady called on us. For a considerable time my wife and I kept saying "Yes Mrs. Solomon, No Mrs. Solomon, and quite-right Mrs. Solomon until finally Mr. Solomon interjected to say "she's a friend, my wife lives in London" This is how we were introduced to a polyandrous society. I recall my wife telling me onetime, she used to be a teacher in a school in Freetown, her lady colleagues would implore upon their husbands,

"I don't mind you playing the field but please keep Friday for me."

I was informed by the General Manager that the Board wanted an interim set of accounts, Profit and Loss and Balance Sheet within three months of my arrival. The company was already in business for three months. This was done and submitted to the board to their satisfaction. Then the day came for the Annual General Meeting. I was at the head table with other members of the board and the accounts were open for discussion. Bedlam broke loose. Members of the audience were on their feet flinging verbal Molotov cocktails at me. Questions, elementary stuff like "How did you value stocks?" Did you adjust for prepayments and accruals?" And on and on it went and I, throughout on my feet. Finally it got so ridiculous and noisy a representative of the auditors (an international firm of accountants) who was present stood up and said these accounts were audited by my firm and we found them satisfactory. "If you have any questions they should be directed to me." With this statement the crowd got quiet. When the white man speaks all listen. Now the question about my ever having attended a board meeting on the ferry made sense.

Jalloh our watchman

I know bribery and corruption is rampant all over the world. But it was here that I came point- blank. We constantly lived in fear of being robbed and we carry this fear to this day. One evening may be around six thirty all dressed up in tuxedo I was about to leave home for a Freemason meeting. I seldom go out in the night. The watchman, the company provided a watchman, who would go to sleep before the family did, asked me in a disturbed tone, "Master you going out?" and I said to him "Yes Jalloh, you watch good O.K?"; "Yes master." He replied.

The next morning I was informed that our neighbor, a First Secretary at the Russian Embassy's house was wiped out clean. Only the refrigerator was left standing. Our houses were along the sea and the thieves had come in a canoe or canoes and taken them all away. The occupants, husband and wife were in the bedroom asleep with the air conditioner going full blast.

The next day when Jalloh turned up for work, I asked him where he was when all this burglary took place. His reply was, "Master anything stolen from your house?"

The plums of office

The Managing Director as part of my duties wanted me routinely to place the orders for coffee with a company in Switzerland who had a representative in Freetown. The first day the rep came to my office we had a pleasant chat and thereafter as this brand of coffee was fast moving I gave him a sizeable order. Before he left he asked me where he should send my commission and I said to him to reduce the invoice cost by that amount. That did not happen.

I noticed during my stay that businesses were in the hands of individual foreigners or foreign owned companies. Sierra Leoneans were completely neglected. I had the authority to allocate quantities of these basic food items to companies and individuals, Sierra Leoneans and foreigners. Wherever and whenever possible I tilted the scales in favor of Sierra Leoneans. I felt that's the least I could do. I gave them substantial allocations.

Around eleven O'clock a Sierra Leonean lady whom I knew very well came into my office and left a huge parcel and dashed off. Jumping up and looking through the window I could see my friend getting into a taxi and was off. It was a parcel of local currency. I took the parcel to the cashier got him to count it make out a receipt for me and credit the amount to her account. I now went to the Managing Director and told him what had taken place and he said, "Mr. Raj she had a lot of money for the first time because of your generous allocations and she wanted you to know she appreciates it. That's the way Mr. Raj they show their appreciation. You should have kept the money."

I used to as a matter of routine work daily after the rest of the staff had left till around six-thirty, seven. The General Manager was vacationing in Las Palmas and I was acting for him. I had the authority to allocate stocks of provisions to the traders. One evening an Indian merchant walks in and after some small talk like your son and my son are class mates and asks how much I am paid and without waiting for an answer takes out a large parcel of British sterling money orders and says to me "This is all yours. All you have to do is to mail it to your bank." This was a time of severe exchange controls and the transfer of funds to overseas was near impossibility. I did not ask him what the quid pro quo was. Disappointed and chagrined he said "Mr. Raj how much do you make here and how much do you think I have?" I was visualizing the trader at his home telling his wife the money he gave me, his son listening to it and repeating it to my son.

Et tu Brute

When the protagonist, jack Burden in Robert Penn Warren's "All The King's Men" is ordered by the corrupt Willie Clark to get something on the "upright judge" Burden protests there can't possibly be "something" on such an honorable man. And Willie Clark demystifies thus.

"There's always something. Man is conceived in sin and born in corruption and he passeth from the stink of the didie to the stench of the shroud, there's always something"

Yes. There is always something.

The National Trading Company (N.T.C.) was the sole importer of basic food stuff such as coffee, tea, onions. The company invited applications for a buying agent, and the bids came in. I was asked by the board to evaluate and recommend one. The managing directors of some of the foreign companies doing business in Freetown were members of the board and they were anxious to win the contract as there was plenty of money to be made. An Indian company called Choithrams had several super markets throughout Sierra Leone selling the same items N.T.C was importing. They had their own Buying office in London. They were among the bidders.

On my vacation in London I visited their London office and the Managing Director requested I give the passports of the three of us – my wife's, my daughter's and mine. Before I could say "Freetown" he had got visas to stop over in Las Palmas in the Canary Islands en route to Sierra Leone. We were met at the airport, cleared through customs and immigration, put up at a classy hotel, taken sightseeing and seen off. A beautiful, beautiful place this Las Palmas!

I recommended Choithrams and they were appointed Buying Agents. Their bid was by far the best; they were familiar with the trade and had an efficient office in London. And yet it barely passes the sniff test.

And so now whenever I listen on television a governor, senator or congressman being taken to task for accepting gifts and favors, I see a finger wagging at me.

About my boss

"Don't worry be happy" kind of guy. This puts the fear of the ghost into you for, should something go amiss you only have yourself to complain to. Women in his office, women in the waiting room, women on the 'phone singing his praises; pray tell me how do you find some time to talk serious work?

As chairman how he conducted board meetings was something to marvel at. A technique that never failed him. The agenda in importance was inversely arranged. The most important was at the bottom. The meeting was to start at 10.30 A.M. and lunch at one P.M. Until eleven, eleven fifteen while waiting for the directors to trickle in he would indulge in small talk and friendly banter. Then the meeting is called to order. Until twelve thirty trivial matters are discussed at length and in excruciating detail. Its twelve thirty now. The directors are now edgy, restless and hungry. He pulls out the big items which are unanimously passed with barely a discussion or dissent.

Our daughter and the N.B. super market in Freetown

I would like to be present when our grandson reads this.

I would pick up our little daughter from school around twelve O'clock and go home for lunch. After she has had her lunch and while asleep I would slip off to office. She would be in the care of Bangura our domestic help. I must mention here Sierra Leoneans are extremely kind to children and elders. They would refer to old folks affectionately as "O man"

On our way home for lunch we have to pass by the N.B. Supermarket where she knows you could get candies. Every-day as we pass the supermarket she would scream to be taken to the supermarket. Think of Ulysses and the sirens. I began to dread that part of the journey. One day as expected when the screaming began I said to Sorie, "Stop the car and put the baby out and we'll go." "No master, no master" he was pleading. "Put her out of the car I said." She was put out of the car. She was so scared she did not utter a peep. I felt she had got the message. Sorie and I independently were wondering what would happen tomorrow. We were passing N.B. and our daughter kept looking at N.B. but no sound.

Inside Track

Coming from Ceylon I know what exchange controls mean. By exchange controls I mean voluminous paper work to be gone through before even a very small amount of local currency can be converted to British pound sterling. I left Ceylon, wife and infant with just ten pounds sterling. Controls over repatriation of funds never get better. They always go in one direction - from bad to worse. The main reason for my leaving Ceylon and working abroad was to earn and save foreign exchange for the education in the English medium of at that time our only child. So when I heard what attorney Johnson casually mention (he was on the board of the Central Bank) during small talk before the board meeting actually began I panicked. He said in a couple of weeks there would be severe controls over the repatriation of funds overseas. As soon as the board lunch was over I walked up to the president of the Indian supermarket chain store close by (yes the very same Choithrams) and explained to him why I need a loan of two thousand pounds sterling. He confirmed the rumor about exchange controls and called the accountant and instructed him to give me two thousand pounds. No agreement and no terms of repayment. With the money I walked up to Barclays Bank of S.L. (all within walking distance) and had the General Manager send the money to my Barclays account in London.

Two or three weeks go by and the nephew of the president comes to my office and makes reference to the loan I had taken and hinted about a bigger allocation for his company. I was mad. I knew it was subtle blackmail. I told him to leave the office, went over to the General Manager of Barclays Bank, Ford whom I knew very well (he has been to our house) and said I need an overdraft of two thousand pounds. He approved it immediately and with the check I went over to the Indian supermarket president's office and handed him the check. He knew nothing at all about it. The next day the young man who spoke to me about the loan was sent by the president to tender his apologies which he did.

In search of a job in Sri Lanka

Ever since I returned to Ceylon from Liberia I wanted to get out again. I lived in the "Customs House" preparing to leave once more. Living in a rented house we kept our acquisitions to bare necessities. Our daughter had difficulty coping with Tamil which was by and large the main medium of communication and instruction at school. I began once again applying for overseas assignments and also tried to find something locally soon. My initial attempts were not successful. Time to get worried! Chandra Zoysa and I served articles in the same firm and have been to several audits together. When you go on an audit with someone you get very friendly. I would take Chandra on my scooter for the audits. Very often I would hear drivers tooting their horns behind me and did not know why until one-day I turned back and saw what was going on. Whenever I stretched my right arm to indicate I would be turning right (at that time these scooters did not gave flashing indicators) Chandra would stretch his left — hence the confusion and tooting of horns.

I heard he was now a big wig in one of the government corporations. I went there with the intension of getting help. When I informed the receptionist I need to see Mr. Zoysa she quite firmly said that is out of the question without an appointment. I said. "Just say Chandraraj is here." I was immediately asked to come up. I noticed there was an armed guard outside his office. After some small talk about what we both have being doing in the interim I told the purpose of my visit. "Chandraraj I was afraid that's why you are here for." Without saying he cannot help me, he said "put my name down as a referee." I later learned that he could not have helped a Tamil however much he would have liked to. I know him. He would have helped me under different circumstances. This hunt for jobs went on for a few more weeks perhaps until I received four good offers. I selected the one with a good salary, car and driver. This was with a civil engineering company.

Leaving Sri Lanka
second time - 1982

All the while I was still hell-bent on getting out of the country. One day an astrologer came to my father – in law's house and I approached him to find out whether I would be getting a job outside the country. He peered into my palm and said not a chance. I got very angry and chased him away. Later one evening while I was walking along the beach I saw the astrologer and ran up to apologize but no sooner he sighted me he took to his heels.

It looked like nothing in the way of an overseas appointment was going to happen. Our daughter was good at swimming and so we entered her for a competition. My wife and I would take her for swimming practices at the Royal College pool. I noticed at the pool the well -known swimmer Tara de Saram giving swimming lessons to children. My wife and I approached her and inquired whether she could coach our daughter. "Sorry I am full up" she replied. After half an hour or so Tara de Saram comes up to us and says I was observing your daughter swim. She has talent "I'll take her on" she said. At the swimming contest she was placed second.

During break we would dash home to have a bite. On one such day there was a cable from my friend Mooly in Sierra Leone to forward my resume for the position of Accountant General of Sierra Leone. It came to pass.

And once again this time four of us, my wife and two children bid Adios to Sri Lanka. My dear, dear parents were shocked. They were convinced we had returned for good.

This was the last time I saw my parents. I never returned to Sri Lanka again.

Accountant General

The position of Accountant General is an exalted one. The entire Treasury of the government of Sierra Leone came under him. All government departments had accountants and sub accountants; the Treasury had accountants and the various provinces had sub accountants and the Accountant general held complete suzerainty over all of them, over two hundred in all. They all reported to the Accountant General. I became the first non-Sierra Leonean Accountant General.

On the first day in my office my secretary (there were two of them) informed me a sub accountant (a lady) from the province wanted to see me. As she came in she left on my table a big parcel and when I inquired what it was she said it was money to buy stuff for my children. I returned the parcel unopened saying give this to your children as a gift from me. I was told it could have been a set up, I do not know for sure. This kind of bold and blatant offers is not unusual in this part of the world. A high official of the Treasury comes to my office and says here is two thousand pounds. It is from a gentleman whom I have seen but never met. She said he gives this every year to the Accountant General. He will not take it back. So I called my secretary and said to her to divvy it up among my staff and the driver at which point the official who brought the money said, "what about me?" and so she too took a share.

As I have mentioned before, a car and driver for an expatriate family is a must. By contract I was promised a car and driver. But none was forthcoming for weeks as I took office as A.G. An official car would pick me up, bring me home for lunch and then drop me off in the evening. This meant my wife and children had no way of getting about. A Ceylonese friend helped us out. This could not go on for-ever. My appointment was made directly by the State House, the office of the president, which meant by the president himself Dr. Siaka Stevens. My appointment was not welcomed by the senior officials of government. So depriving me of a car was a way of getting even and also a way of showing their importance. On Mondays all the high officials like the Governor of the Central Bank, Financial Secretary, the Deputy Financial Secretary and the Accountant General meet with the president at State House to review the activities of the Accountant General's Department and that of the Central Bank. This became necessary because fraud and abuse had been discovered in the A.G's department.

My visit to the State House

This was my first visit to the State House where we were to meet with the President. It's always on Monday morning at 10.O'Clock. I did not have a car and so got a ride from the Deputy Financial Secretary. Those attending the meeting on this day were Governor of the Central Bank, the Financial Secretary, Deputy Financial Secretary and I. We arrived at the State House well ahead of time. At 10 O'clock we were called in. There were chairs lined up opposite the president's desk. They were far from ostentatious.

(To say not ostentatious and leave it at that would be misleading; I have seen the president being driven along Lumley beach in a British M.G. sports which was then out of production, custom built especially for him)

When the president walked in we all stood up and sat down after he had taken his seat. There was complete silence, a kind of speak only when you are spoken to code of conduct prevailed. Those at the meeting appeared very nervous thinking twice, measuring their words before they spoke. The president asked how each department was faring and was told everything was honky-dory. I was seated on the extreme left of the president which meant he had to turn his head to address me. He did so and asked in a general way "How is our accountant?" I had may be ten seconds. I blurted out "No Car". He turned to the Financial Secretary and feigning surprise in high decibel remarked, "What no car for accountant?" On my return to the Treasury the same day I was given a budget and told to select any car I wished.

Left to stew

As I have said before the top officials of government did not take kindly to me. This is an important position and they preferred one of their own to occupy it. My initial contract of employment was for two years. A decision must have been taken by them to run the clock and give me no work. I was seated in my office with hardly anything to do. All the work that I should be doing was being done by the Deputy Financial Secretary. He was a London qualified accountant. This cannot go on I felt.

The staff of the entire government service in matters of leave, promotions and transfers came under the purview of the Establishment Secretary (E.S.). I requested an appointment with the E.S. I was asked to come over immediately. His office was across the road. I mentioned to him that no work is passed on to me and I am idling. He listened to me patiently and said, "This is not the first time they have been doing this. You go I'll handle this." This must have come as a shock to those who were working against me. The brass of this guy! From now on I began working as an Accountant General should. For the first time in the history of the department with the help and active cooperation of my staff I was able to produce an Income and Expenditure report for the whole country which impressed the International Monitory Fund officials as they now had something to work with.

About my boss

Tall and heavily set, self confidence oozed out of every pore of his body. A bear with a laser like mind. An intellectual bonanza to watch him dribble like Pele around the minds of the members of the International Monetary Fund from Washington. And he enjoyed it.

Mums the word

I noticed in Sierra Leone a trend. Certain decisions are taken by my superiors concerning me but no reasons are given for such actions. Not even your subordinates will let you into the reason. In the week I arrived in Freetown as Accountant of the National Trading Company I was requested to appear in courts to explain the accounting system prevailing as a member of the staff was being charged for theft. I studied the accounting system and appeared before the magistrate. I was sworn in and after preliminary questions the court adjourned. The following day my boss said I don't need to appear again. No reasons were given. This happened again. The Accountant General signs all checks for the government. There is always a rush by individuals high and low to obtain their checks in the least possible delay. A commission was appointed by the President's office to inquire into the way payments are processed and checks signed as there had been complaints of delay. I was the chief witness. It was open to the public and the press. There was quite a gathering. I appeared along with my two deputies Naloo and Banya Sierra Leoneans both. I was asked many questions which I thought I answered adequately. Then came the question, If there were checks to be signed by you and among them one from the president's office which one I was asked I would sign first. I said the one from the president's office. I was not asked why? The next day I was told I don't need to attend the commission any more. No reasons were given.

On crying

Crying I suppose is quite normal. It is expected. We begin life on this planet bawling. If we do not cry the midwife will slap our bottoms and make us cry. Most of the time we forget why and when we cried. There must remain in the memory of most people occasions when they cried and they felt they had no more tears to shed.

There were three occasions I cried I can never forget.

The time I cried when my parents left me at Chunnakam station and departed for Malaysia I have already recounted.

The National Trading Company where I was Accountant got into financial difficult times. The reason - without warning the president "influenced" by expatriate companies that imported what the N.T.C was importing solely, removed the monopoly that N.T.C. enjoyed. N.T.C had large stocks of onions, tomato paste, coffee and other food items and more were on order. As soon as the monopoly was removed without warning private companies placed their orders directly with their overseas suppliers and refused to buy from N.T.C. Food stuff began to rot and had to be dumped or sold well below cost.

I knew I had to soon find a job. I was applying all over with no success. Then my friend Mooly who was working in Sierra Leone called me to say there was a vacancy in a British mining company, a very reputable one and that he was not interested and suggested I apply. I knew the chief accountant. He would come to my office and while the two of us spun yarns all the provisions would be loaded into his truck. The mining company was located in the provinces far from Freetown where I worked. I applied and was called for an interview. I had to travel by bus and a hotel was booked.

On my way to the board room for the interview I saw the chief accountant standing in the premises and he gave me the thumps up. I knew at this point the job was in the bag. The interviewing board comprised of one Sierra Leonean and I think two Brits. The interview went very well. It was easy to tell from the questions that were lobbed to me and their responses to my replies. Then one member of the board a Brit asked me how I got the job at the National Trading Company. And I replied "kissing goes by favor." There was dead silence. The interview ended. I spent the night at the hotel. No one from the company came to see me and in the morning I left for home in Freetown.

My wife and daughter were in London. Back home in Freetown I cried and cried and cried. I fell on my knees and cried. How could I have been so stupid, so puerile? A wonderful job with a big pay and huge benefits thrown away. I had sacrificed the future of the whole family by my silliness. Ever since, I have been extremely cautious at interviews not to shoot my mouth.

Beat me kick me don't touch my child

What is most unbearable for every parent is to see his or her child in distress. My mother, a Jaffna Hindu, rural conservative woman took to smoking (I know the brand "Bristol" nicotine-wise the lightest one can light up) because she could not go to sleep due to her child having got into difficulties at school.

Our daughter did not have a Green Card at this time. Consequently she could not apply for jobs which she was absolutely keen on and well qualified for it. She was in distress and my wife and I were painfully aware of this. If there was any way we could have helped we would have jumped at it. It was beyond our control. If by money or manual effort it could have been resolved we would have gladly done it. I would grieve constantly over this and so did my wife. Grieve on the train to work, at home, everywhere, every waking hour. It was just unbearable. My wife and I carried this sorrow for a very long time. It was a time of pain and anguish, disappointment and fear, the constant what next?

My first job in the United States

Directly from the position of Accountant General (A.G) of the Government of Sierra Leone assisted by two deputies and two secretaries, where secretaries to ministers of state would come to my office pleading to have their ministers' checks for travel and reimbursement of expenditure signed, direct line to the president's office, attended opening of parliament where prominent seats on a dais were allocated to the A.G. and his two deputies, had his own private toilet and bathroom, car and chauffeur round the clock, security at the residence to name a few envious perks. I recall when Sierra Leone was having restrictions on the repatriation of funds overseas and overseas travel was kept to a minimum I received a telephone call from my wife's brother that my father-in-law had passed away. My wife had to travel to Ceylon for the funeral which means funds have to be released for the tickets tout de suite. I went to the Finance Minister's office upstairs. At that time fortunately the Governor of the Central Bank was in his office. I was invited in right away and when they heard my urgent need on the advice of the Finance Minister the Governor ordered funds be released forthwith. It was from this prestigious position that I came to my first job in the United States of America.

In this narrative certain names and identifying characteristics have been changed, but the events are retold just as it happened as I recall it.

While in Freetown Sierra Leone my close British pal Vincent who was attached to my department released by the United Kingdom government warned me that things will be quite different in America. I did not give it much thought at that time. The company (let's call it) Narotam Systems was located in Connecticut. I was given by the company a week off to attend to personal matters. Throughout my stay in Africa I had a driver and so did very little driving. The roads were narrow and cars moved slowly. The company was off Merritt Parkway and I was intimidated by the speed of the traffic. My Brother-in –Law supervised my first dry run to the office prior to starting work and cautioned me that I should do at least forty miles per hour as he observed I was on a "break-neck" thirty five. At the end of it he wanted to know whether I would like another shot at it and we did another run.

During the weeks' vacation prior to starting work I met the chief of personnel who with his deputy took me to lunch at the company cafeteria. I was so nervous I picked a sandwich and said that would do. At the end of the lunch we carried our trays to dislodge the left-over food into the trash bin when the chief of personnel cautioned me with a giggle that I should dump only the food and spare the tray.

As I drove into the parking lot on the first day I got the willies. I saw a sea of cars. I had never seen anything like this before. There were at this time three thousand employees and together with the maintenance crew and visitors it was even more. Hurriedly I parked at the first opening I saw. On leaving after work I could not spot my car. Security arrived and wanted to know whether I parked on the east or west side. I had no clue. They then put me in the jeep and took me round the parking lot and asked that I spot the car. Henceforth I would park the car close to the helicopter landing pad.

There was security at the entrance to the building. I notified security at the entrance of my arrival and he informed the accounts department the new man is here. A gentleman came to fetch me. I was photographed and a name tag given which like all the others had to be worn at all times while in the building. There was a green dot on my badge which the others did not. It took me many months to summon sufficient gumption to ask the reason for this. I was told it was to indicate I was a non-national.

I was informed by my superior that I cannot under any circumstances leave my department which was approximately the size of two large bedrooms. If I had to go to the toilet for a pee or a poo I should be accompanied by some- one from the department. They would stand outside of course. There were private security officials all over the building. On my arrival in the morning I should call the accounts department and someone will come down to fetch me. I worked under these conditions for over eighteen months. I was under extreme stress. From a private toilet and bath to not be able to pee unless accompanied by a colleague was very humiliating. I could hear the words ball and chain being uttered. There were days we worked late which meant the stress from confinement was even more. Initially I would consume prunes before leaving home which further exacerbated my poo problems especially. I gave up eating prunes. I was told that Narotam Systems was a defense contractor and only citizens were allowed to work for security reasons. Hence the need to take these extra ordinary stringent security measures.

A lady from personnel came to the accounts department and drove me to the immigration office in Norwalk to straighten out matters relating to my visa. She accomplished it efficiently. Before returning to work I suggested we have a cup of coffee and she gladly agreed. We ducked into a restaurant had our coffee and just before I got into the car for the return trip she remarked, "You talk funny." This was in August of 1985.

I meet this gentleman at the gym four days a week. We are friends. As two families we have had meals in each- others' homes and this Easter he brought for me only delicious goodies. He is a successful high school football coach. He liked my books on Shakespeare and on Humor. About a month ago he tells me, "Chandra you talk funny." This in May of 2014. The tribal marks of the first generation, the dregs, the sediment, hang-ups immigrants of bi-culture bring from the old to the new country.

I now understand what Arianne Huffington, founder of Huffington Post, president of the Oxford University students union in London meant when she remarked at a symposium (I am paraphrasing) I prefer to write than give a speech.

On the first day at Narrotam Systems I was given a ledger with many bank accounts, relevant bank statements and asked to reconcile. There was absolutely no guidance. The books were bound differently and I had difficulty making sense of the numbers. So I sat and worked at it day after day and as soon as I finished one month the next lot of statements for the following month would arrive. Bank reconciliations everywhere is done by a junior accounts clerk. Here you have the Accountant General of Sierra Leone doing nothing but bank reconciliations all day and at times into the night. Back in Sierra Leone at the Treasury there was a bank reconciliation department reporting to me.

It was pretty obvious to me I was not wanted here and my presence was an irritation. I was on a high salary, very likely much more than most of those in my department. The payroll guy had leaked this confidential information for he too must have been upset. He poisoned my life at Narrotam Systems at the well-head. One day it was snowing pretty bad and 'Jane' in my department tells me "Chandra you will never get lost in the snow." alluding to my midnight complexion. Amidst the blur of these dark days, two colleagues 'Mannie' with whom I correspond weekly and 'Spat' whose family are friends of mine stood out like lighthouses. I mentioned to Mannie what Jane had said about being lucky I will never get lost in the snow and her immediate reaction was, "you think that was funny?" This was a time personal computers were being introduced and lessons were conducted in Excel and the department was one computer short and so Mannie and I would share. We got very friendly. The other was, Spat who would during lunch time keep me company within the closed confines of the department and at times take me for a spin in his car with the C.B. on, intercepting truckers' very colorful conversation.

One day noticing there was no one around, it was lunch time and in urgent to relieve myself I walked a few yards from my department and went to the toilet. As I emerged there was the security guy walking by. He noticed I was unescorted. With a broad grin he took me to my department and there by which time my supervisor had arrived and I was handed over. I was warned if this happened again it could be serious. My friend Spat, observing all this said he would be only too happy to accompany me to the toilet. All I need to do is ask. Thank you Spat you are not always around during lunch time when I needed to pee or when like Napoleon should I be attacked from behind.

It was time for my annual review. The supervisor and I alone were in the board room. He gave me a form to read and sign. Glancing quickly I noticed he had commented that my English leaves much to be desired. I was furious. I protested I will not sign this. I said, "Dill you can select anyone in this company and put the two of us in this room and give any subject to write an essay on and I am certain I will do better." He could not believe his ears. "I'll have to speak to the manager." So saying he walked off with my review. He later came up to me and said that I should write something for the manager to judge. Grabbing paper and pen and in an agitated frame of mind, this is what I submitted:

I have always received high praise for my written communication. On numerous occasions I have drafted for the managing director of the company I have been employed in the annual report to the share- holders. I excel in it and

Business letters have been my forte. Given the circumstances, I have the ability to temper my written communication to suit the occasion. Be down- right matter of fact or diplomatic as deem fit.

In the circumstances you will appreciate 'Dill', not only do I disagree with the comments in cage- K, but also feel somewhat disappointed which of course is a personal matter.

One swallow' Dill' does not make a summer.

5/14/87.

Back to bank reconciliation which is all I was given to do through- out my service at this company. Long before I arrived there was a twenty five cents difference in the Chemical Bank reconciliation. Now this became the monkey on my back throughout my tenure at this company. Every now and then my supervisor would ask "Haven't you yet found the twenty five cent difference?" I was kept on a twenty five cent leash. My predecessor had been carrying this twenty five cents difference for many months. On the day I was leaving Narrotam Systems and while the bank reconciliation job was being handed back to the guy from whom I inherited it, right under my nose the Supervisor wrote off the twenty five cents difference.

I could not take my troubles to personnel. To do so I will have to get permission from my supervisor and he must provide escort. There will be too many questions. I knew he could put an end to my working in this company and I was carrying too many responsibilities to risk that.

I was going on vacation to Canada the following day. My supervisor minutes before closing came to me with the gentleman who was doing the bank reconciliation for months before me to check on my work before departure. The twenty five cents came up again. I do not remember what I said but it was sufficient to provoke him to prod on my chest with his index finger. This infuriated me and I spoke aloud in anger. The mouse actually roared. Stepped upon the worm will turn. I do not recall the words but it was enough for the manager to come flying out of the room to see what was going on. When he saw three of us he walked past us.

Most bad things happen to you when you are on vacation. All the plotting can be done freely. In my absence the supervisor and his buddies must have realized the finger jabbing was out of order. They must have felt I would take the matter with personnel which I was not going to. On my return I was informed I will have to leave in a month. I was on a work visa. I alone was authorized to work. I had a wife and two children depending on me. My foreign qualification and working experience amounted to cipher.

Let me say this about my time at Narrotam Systems. They were to put it mildly difficult days, I was weak, afraid and submissive berated and bullied (that Faustian choice again keeps haunting me) Many have asked me how on earth did I cope. I suppose time partially reconciles us to anything. I gradually became settled, doggedly settled, reluctantly settled as a wild animal would be in a cage. Many a time I pondered over the animal mentality of fight or flight but chose the third to stay as anything else was unthinkable and yet I did not think I was the Mozart of misfortune or Paganini of poor luck. I was fully aware of my shortcomings and did nada to combat it.

These were days that drove me into the embrace of Bacchus. Days that pained my adoring wife and loving son who was attending high school at that time. Several times I felt I had reached the very limits of endurance. As Frank McCourt described it, job at this time was "death without dignity." During this period I lost sight of myself. I was in a state of acute delirium. The foundation on which I stood was solid – the feeling that I was doing it for the family, a feeling of pride and a determination to see it through. Now all the bad days are behind me. The angel of forgetfulness and forgiveness has gathered up and carried away much of the misery and all the bitterness of those sad and turbulent times. Perhaps we must accept that at times life falls dead like a dough instead of soaring away like a balloon into the colors of the sunset as we would have liked.

About my boss

Little guy – in intellect a Lilliput, in hauteur a Gulliver. Very insecure in his position. Bullied staff into submission. A bachelor with no other interest, lived with his mother, came in late and worked till around eight in the night when dinner would be ready.

Supervisors and managers are every day human beings like every- one else. They go to extremes to survive and during that journey conscience atrophies at a rapid clip.

I was on the road again tramping the streets in search of a job with responsibilities undiminished.

My second job in the United States

Once more the popular East Coast pediatric neurologist rides into town and rescues the family from dire straits. I get a job in a reinsurance audit firm in Manhattan. About reinsurance I did not know my nose from my elbow. The office is on 44th East whistling distance from Grand Central Station is a two hour door to door by Metro North one way. The owner asks me whether I don't mind the commute and I say with casual ease, "No problem." I needed the job.

It's far from straight forward. I leave home in Shelton at 5.30 in the morning and take the 6.25 train from Bridgeport - sun, snow, winter or warm weather. I know auditing; I have done it before. Say Reinsurance? That's a completely different breed of cat. I promise to myself (as I have done countless times before) "I will read up." "I will get up in the morning and study" "I will devote every minute of the train commute to studies." Nothing like that happened. When I get home I am too tired. As soon as I board the train and take the regular corner window seat (every regular has his place and seldom would any one poach) I fall into a deep slumber only to be awoken at the Grand Central Terminal by noisy disembarking commuters. Sometimes I am joined by my friend Selva at Fairfield station when we will natter for a while and agree with a wordless nod to knock it off.

This goes on for a few years until one day the president/owner calls me up and says "find another job." The sword of Damocles falls again. My son is in Australia on an exchange scholarship. Do you think this is the ideal time to be without a job? Try again. So I go up to the big man and plead that he gives me a few months. "No can do" he says. Be on your way. I ask him whether he would service my health insurance for a few months. He agrees and changes his mind.

About my boss

A lion to his staff, a lamb to all who handed jobs to his company, was at the feet of the powerful and at the throat of the weak. Came in a foul mood Monday mornings and wary of going home on Friday evenings. He would talk work and work and very little else. "Why do you need to see a movie when you can be doing office work" was his way of thinking. Could never understand how people can have fun ....they should be reading about the work at hand. He had the charm of an undertaker and the charisma of a corpse. An excellent memory, could remember numbers to two decimal places. Never misses an opportunity to brag about the small beginnings of his company of which he is now chairman with the staff "oohing" and 'aahing" and drooling in chorus.

My third job in the United States

You guessed it. The pediatric neurologist rides in to the rescue. I join 'the Institute' a 501 C (3) organization. I accompanied the big man to Surinam (South America) on a mission, made me Director of Finance and everything goes super- duper; everything goes swimmingly well. Timely accounts to the satisfaction of the board, ah life could not better be. Rapid salary increases - (May 1995 – $31,000.00; November 1995- $45,000.00; May 1996 - $52,000.00; May 1997-$ 58,000 excluding attractive bonuses.) It happened again. My wife and I went to London on a vacation - I had not taken one for a long time. During my absence the president and sycophants on the staff feel they can get someone cheaper. How did I know this? I will tell you presently. This is the bane of capitalism.

The president comes into my office and leaves a type written note and walks away. The note announces to the staff that I will be *retiring* as of 8/15/98. On a hand scribble on the note, "I need a letter from you too informing me that you are retiring" An obvious devious ploy proprietors adopt to dodge paying unemployment benefits and any claim of compensation. I take a copy of it and with the typed note go to his office and return his note saying I cannot do it. Thereafter I sent copies of it to members of the Board who were totally in the dark of these entire "cloak and dagger" goings on. On my way out when I went to shake the hand of a Kahuna she tells me we are hiring a book-keeper on a very low salary. A few months later the Institute went belly-up.

About my boss

Quintessential salesman with a perennial smile that is disarming. As Pedro said in "Much ado about nothing" "from the crown of his head to the soul of his foot he is all mirth" He could jolly any one out of his (or her) blues. The kind of companion you want to have in your car on a cross country journey. Even when he harms you he can do it with such finesse and charm, you feel he has done you a great favor. I have witnessed many a cashiered staff give him an affectionate parting hug. A blue beard easily bored with the routine and responsibilities of family life, the current spouses never suspecting that he had an excess of exes.

Was able at the same time talk serious business on the telephone; read an important memo making corrections; compulsively moving things around on his desk; flash smiles at all those ambling in and out of his office and observing everything going on around him.

The visceral need, the pathological imperative to please all his staff all the time compounded by his affliction with the Clara Bow Syndrome – the inability to say **No -** made him a lousy manager which, not surprisingly led to the early demise of his career, and the collapse of the institution he dearly loved.

Attributes of a good boss

After five years of articles (accountancy) with a prestigious international firm of Chartered Accountants in Sri Lanka (Ceylon) working in three continents, in over a dozen companies, serving as many bosses and bossing over many for over four decades, looking after other people's money like a well paid security guard, emerging with a clear conscience, clean hands and fingers unburned, honed on the wheel of personal experience as victor and vanquished (you catch some; you miss some) here in random order are in my opinion the attributes I would look for in a good boss.

- Never shift the blame for any failure to your subordinate. You are the boss.
- Never take credit for your subordinate's good work. Send the word round, "It was Charlie who did it all"
- Defend your staff against outsiders' complaints but tell them forcefully where they have gone wrong and what future consequences would be.
- Be one jump ahead about their annual increments. Do not wait for your staff to remind you. They love their families too.
- Recognize good work.
- Observe all the rules yourself.

- Delegate and monitor progress. Do not be needling over trifles.
- Let the staff know you are firm but fair with no favorites.
- If a member of the staff wishes to discuss something personal give him or her, an earnest hearing. Do not shoo- them away.
- Let your instructions be precise, brief, devoid of double entendre.
- When you make a mistake admit it without glossing over it. Do not under estimate your staff's intelligence.
- Get along with your own boss. Else, those below you will by-pass you and you will be reduced to irrelevancy.
- Perform in a way when you leave your office, you will be leaving it better than when you arrived. Even though with the passage of time this too will pass.
- If you have to convey bad news, do it yourself without assigning it to your deputy.
- Be able to say "No" when the demands are out of bounds. You are not running for the office of the president of the United States of America.

A fair question

In the light of what I have listed as attributes of a good boss the reader is justified in asking: "You have been a boss yourself. Is there anything you wish to tell us?

Yes. One incident sticks out like a festering sore thumb which after all these many years has not cured. So let me warm my old age with the memory of my own sinfulness.

It was within six months, may be three of my taking office as Accountant General. One of my two deputies had reached the mandatory retirement age of fifty five. An employee could get a one year extension, no more, if the head of department recommended it. This deputy of mine in question side stepped me and applied directly to the Establishment Secretary's office that routinely dealt with staff matters. The Establishment Secretary's Office sent the papers to me for my recommendation following set procedure.

I declined and his application was turned down. He did not talk to me before, during or after this for him life changing drama was being played out.

Did I decline because my ego was bruised? You be the judge.

I have been asked numerous times

Why don't you want to go to Sri Lanka? Close friends and members of my family have asked this question many, many times and now for the first time I am asking myself seriously the same question. Throughout this narrative I have striven to be faithful to Joe Friday's admonition "Just the facts Ma'am"

I lived in Ceylon without interruption for 22 years.

During the 22 year period, before I was ceremoniously married in 1967 having legally registered in 1966, I was human flotsam and jetsam drifting without direction. At the Jaffna College boarding in Vaddukoddai; at my uncles' during school vacation wherever they were employed; briefly with my parents in Ratnakara Place, Dehiwela until in 1958 with the communal riots when they decided to "emigrate" to Chankanai their home in Jaffna. Drift wood again. Resident at the Central Y.M.C.A in Fort; at a boarding on 676 Galle Road Bambalapitiya; another boarding on 18 Visaka Road, Bambalapitiya and thereafter for about 8 years I lived in the home of my friend's uncle and aunt at

84 Fussels Lane, Wellawatte until I married in 1967. Left Ceylon for Sierra Leone in 1972

In what follows I am merely answering the question why I do not wish to visit Sri Lanka. It is a subjective reaction. I am dumb enough to know to every point of view there is the obverse and reverse, recto and verso sides to it. And there will be as many views as there are readers. It may even set off a hocus-pocus of criticism elicit cryptic responses, critical approval or censure.

Throughout my residency in Colombo I never felt comfortable. I would go further and say I felt insecure. I a Tamil was linguistically and culturally separate and gradually becoming unequal to the Sinhalese. Worse still, the naked absence of the sanctity of law, a law wherein citizens of civilized nations look for sanctuary had gone on permanent vacation. Beneath the pretentious patina of respectability and illusive placid calm waters of daily life I sensed a roiling undercurrent of hostility between the two major communities, the Sinhalese and the Tamils which reached its apogee in the riots of 1958. My father who had paid a deposit to buy land and build a home for us in Ratmalana had to abandon the project in a hurry and hightail to Jaffna, then the traditional Tamilian territory.

When Mrs. Bandarnaike swept to power on the hunched backs of the rural masses, hunched by years of neglect by the affluent and the elite, there was a volcanic eruption of Sinhala mainly Buddhist demonstrative patriotism. The morning after the Bandaranike victory I was in my cubicle at Hunters. Ariyaratne a clerk in my department who would normally send word through a peon whether he could see me on matters official or personal walked unannounced into my office, his chest full blown and said "Mr. Chandraraj we are in power now" and walked out. From the tone and tenor of his body language I realized he was not making a social call.

When a white man in the United States calls a black man a nigger he would very often genuinely without pretense claim "I have close African American friends." So too my close friends at this time were Sinhala Buddhists, Noel Fernando and, Chandra Zoysa who later became Treasurer of the United National Party.

The Elephant Pass was the Maginot Line, the Mason Dixon Line that separated the Sinhala south from the Tamil north. "Yarl Devi" is the train that carried the Tamils from the capital Colombo to Jaffna. The moment the train crossed Elephant Pass I have seen Tamils shed their pants and slip into "Verti" in which they were at home. Once I arrived in my mother's village home of Chankanai I felt free. Like a fish caught by an angler was thrown back into the sea. The cultural and linguistic affinity would sweep all over me like a cool, colossal wave on the beach. Communication and interaction was effortless. Whereas in Colombo when I entered a shop to buy something the shopkeeper who was Sinhala and frequently not fluent in English, I had to tortuously explain in blatantly faulty Sinhala what I wanted; in Jaffna I did not have that problem of being understood, or for that matter here in the United States.

When I returned to Sri Lanka from Liberia the four of us lived in Thalakotuwa Gardens in Borella. This was early 1980. My wife's teacher colleague at St Thomas College, Mount Lavinia and her husband were going to be in Australia for a while and we rented their apartment. Around eight o' clock one night the front door was open and a man walked right in and wanted to know where the telephone was and before I could answer he spotted the telephone, walked up to it, dialed someone, spoke in rapid Sinhala, placed the phone back on the wall and walked out like a breeze. What could have I done? Call the police? Challenge him? This man knew I wouldn't dare and he was right. I didn't dare.

To quote Falstaff in Shakespeare's Henry the Fourth:

"The better part of valor is discretion, in which the better part *I have saved my life.*"

We are moved and molded not by altruistic patriotism and the distant scene of one nation under god but by the pin pricks of day-to-day living.

In parenthesis may I reflect that having lived everywhere and nowhere perhaps that's another reason I do not have the anchors of sentiment and nostalgia to bind me to Sri Lanka the land of my forbears.

My parents have passed away and my only sibling lives in New Zealand. Our two children are in good jobs, have chosen their spouses wisely and are happy together. We "gave away" our daughter and son but have got them back as loving granddaughter and grandson. "Fair exchange" my grandmother would say "is no robbery." I slice my day three ways – home - gym - library all within sneezing distance of each other. I am having a whale of a time.

My Sri Lanka passport is franked: Departed 19/1/1982.

So dear friends and family - for me its "Sayonara Sri Lanka"

Summing up

Have climbed the Eifel tower twice, been twice round the canal in Amsterdam, have visited Geneva, Zurich. London, Rome, Singapore, Spain, Sydney and Perth, the Taj Mahal, Toronto and more but what I remember most is not the pleasure from my travels but the pain of looking for jobs. The question I have to ask myself is what went wrong buster?

I do not need a Sigmund Freud to provide the answer.

I tried to get by in a fast changing supersonic first world with a snail pace third world knowledge and paid a painfully heavy emotional price.

And so my advice to my grandchildren is this:

Keep abreast with the latest – technology and academia.

When do you know life has completed a full circle?

When the child whose hand you held tight when crossing the road now picks your bags off the car; when the child you bathed and dressed in the morning and then to school and back; when you had watched your child safely across oceans and over continents through the Sturm und Drang of communal riots, tribal clashes and coup d' et tats cautions the parents to bring her infant child in a stroller safely home from a twenty minute stroll round the block you know then life has happily come a full circle and the dots have been joined.

The parents have earned the right to settle back and unwind. God's in heaven and all's well with the world.

End Notes

Writing this narrative set in motion a powerful search mechanism and one of its satisfactions was that it allowed me to come to terms with my outer and inner self. It allowed me to work through life's hardest knocks, disappointments, failures, it helped to find understanding and solace. A certain malaise envelopes one's whole being when reflecting on the past in the present. There was a tendency to look over my shoulder, to painfully ponder whether I am casting people in a biased, fallacious and unreasonable light but once again I take comfort from the belief that this is my story, these are the facts as I know them and this is how I remember them.

So much time has rolled by so much churning water under the George Washington Bridge since these events occurred, I will be an outright fool if I should harbor any ill will towards those with whom I disagreed. "Only a fool in his folly may think he can turn the wheel on which he turns." This is how it was meant to be.

If there is a consistent theme in this book, it is the discovery of my limitations and learning to live with them making no effort to overcome them. The recognition of one's limitations is painful. The career I chose or that which was made for me by fate, karma, circumstance, whatever name you care to call it served to expose my limitations. I am glad I was able to achieve so much with so little.

I have recorded my past just as I remembered it; used no fictional devices beyond reconstructing events from memory; have not blended characters, manipulated events or bent chronology to add luster to my narrative - I have no need for it for I have arrived at that point of time in my life when I can see and feel my left hand clinging to the cradle of hope while the right nervously stretching to the crematorium walls of mortality.

I would like to conclude with Huck in "Huckleberry Finn" –

"(s) o there ain't nothing more to write about, and I am rotten glad of it, because if I'd a known what a trouble it was to make a book I wouldn't a tackled it and ain't going to no more."

You see I have finished the book. (Stone the crows!) Now the book and I are going to be famous for ever.

September 16, 2014